IN SEARCH
of a WAY OUT

A TRUE STORY OF BULLYING, DEPRESSION, *and a* JOURNEY TOWARD HOPE

BOBBY STRAUS
Illustrated By Michael Ferguson

POLAR LIGHTS

Greenwood Village, Colorado

In Search of a Way Out: A True Story of Bullying, Depression, and a Journey Toward Hope
Published by Polar Lights Publishing, LLC
Greenwood Village, Colorado

ISBN: 978-1-7346785-0-5

BIOGRAPHY & AUTOBIOGRAPHY/Personal Memoirs
Psychology/Mental Health
Young Adult Nonfiction/Social Topics/Bullying

PUBLISHER'S CATALOGING-IN-PUBLICATION DATA
Names: Straus, Bobby, author.
Title: In search of a way out : a true story of bullying, depression, and a journey toward hope / Bobby Straus.
Description: First trade paperback original edition. | Greenwood Village [Colorado] : Polar Lights Publishing, LLC, 2020. Also being published as an ebook.
Identifiers: ISBN 978-1-7346785-0-5
Subjects: LCSH: Autobiography. | Depression in men. | Bullying. | Self-esteem.
BISAC: BIOGRAPHY & AUTOBIOGRAPHY / Personal Memoirs. | PSYCHOLO-GY / Mental Health. | YOUNG ADULT NONFICTION / Social Topics/Bullying.
Classification: LCC CT275 | DDC 813.6 STRAUS—dc22

Interior design by Victoria Wolf, Wolf Design and Marketing

QUANTITY PURCHASES: Schools, companies, professional groups, clubs, and other organizations may qualify for special terms when ordering quantities of this title. For information, email bobby@bobbystraus.com.

For Francesca and Jack

Mental pain is less dramatic than physical pain, but it is more common and also much harder to bear.

The frequent attempt to conceal mental pain increases the burden.

It is easier to say, "My tooth is aching," than to say, "My heart is broken."

—C.S. Lewis, "The Problem of Pain"

CONTENTS

PART ONE
UNMASKED

PROLOGUE

Is there no way out of the mind?
—Sylvia Plath

What if your greatest challenge in life is a disease that you do not know you have?

What if the disease has a mind of its own that controls your life, and you have no idea that it is pulling the strings of all your decisions?

What if the symptoms of the disease are so subtle that as they progress, you are unaware they are destroying your life and the lives of the ones you love?

What if the disease starts early in your childhood, making you emotionally vulnerable and prone to being abused or victimized?

What if the disease is not physical, but mental? How do you recognize a disease that hides in your mind? How do you find someone who can help you if the effects of the disease shut down your emotions, disabling your ability to think clearly or ask the right questions?

What if your self-talk is negative because of the disease, and you continuously feel defeated, overwhelmed, insignificant, and unworthy? How do you cope with reality?

What if the disease is so good at hiding itself that if it goes untreated, one of the potential outcomes for your life is self-destruction?

For many people, this disease is their reality.

For nearly fifty years, it was my reality.

The disease is depression.

This book is my contribution to those who are suffering but looking for hope—for themselves or for someone they love.

INTRODUCTION

Depression is the most unpleasant thing I have ever experienced. It is that absence of being able to envisage that you will ever be cheerful again. The absence of hope. That very deadened feeling, which is so very different from feeling sad. Sad hurts but it's a healthy feeling. It is a necessary thing to feel. Depression is very different.

—J.K. Rowling

How can I get out of here? I have been asking myself that question for most of my life.

For me, "here" was not a physical place, but the mental and emotional prison of clinical depression that I was born into, and from which, for years, I thought there was no escape. The walls of my prison were not made of brick or stone, but of emotions and conflicted thoughts and beliefs. I was a prisoner in my mind, trying to escape.

This book journals my battle with depression, the effects of having been bullied in my childhood, and how I eventually made it beyond my prison walls.

It has been said that of all the things that can adversely affect a person's happiness, there is nothing more troubling and damaging than a person's negative thoughts and beliefs. This is especially true when a person is born into life conditions in which they have a predisposition to mental health challenges.

Some people have genetic disadvantages that can affect their mental health, while others may be vulnerable to biological factors. For others, being raised in an emotionally unsafe or abusive environment can be impactful. And then there are those who have all of these unfavorable conditions. In each of these situations, the result is the same: a person grows up without having learned how to cope with the everyday trials and tribulations of life, without fully experiencing happiness, laughter and love and without the energy to pursue a life of meaning and purpose. The consequences can be devastating, as it was for me.

Even as the disease undermines our ability to maintain mental clarity and weakens our emotional stability, we struggle to be a functioning member of society. Day after day, we put on our happy, everything-is-fine mask—which we hide behind—to create the appearance that all is well; life is good. But keeping that mask on is a lonely and exhausting endeavor. And worrying about somebody finding out who is behind it—frightening.

I was once that lonely and fearful person wearing a mask and hiding in plain sight. For most of my life, I didn't know that I suffered from depression—but I knew something was wrong, and I did my best to deny it and hide it.

I am not alone in my struggles. There are millions of people with mental health challenges who live in emotional isolation and do not know what to do. As you read the pages that follow, you may discover that my story reminds you of someone you know—someone close to you, who you love, who is silently crying for help. You may be that person who is wearing a mask, hiding, and searching for answers to understand the different shades of darkness in your mind.

As I share my story, I want to help lift the curtain on the taboo of depression and give others the courage to find help and be freed from their prison.

Depression is an incredibly difficult subject to read, talk, and write about; yet over the past fifty years, I have come to understand all too well why this subject is, for the most part, swept under the rug.

If it has taken me five decades to muster up the courage to face my demons and eventually share my experience about living with the disease, how could I ever expect anybody else to embrace the idea of wanting to read about depression?

I have come to learn that if those of us who suffer, or have suffered, from depression keep our experiences hidden away, the stigma associated with the illness is never going to end. That, in a nutshell, is the reason I finally decided to write this book.

While I do not pretend to think there is something unique or special about me, I do nevertheless hope that by sharing my story I can play a small part in helping someone else who is suffering from this crippling disease to confront their illness and find their path to being healed.

If you are a family member or a friend of someone who battles depression, I promise, by the end of this book, you will be able to understand what is happening to them and why they so desperately need your help. I also promise that the insight you take away from this book will ease the frustration and hopelessness you experience living with a family member or being around a friend, or any other person who lives with depression. Inasmuch as the disease is destructive to those who have it, it also takes a heavy toll on those who must deal with that person. There is plenty of suffering to go around. Nobody is at fault.

So, what is at the heart of this book? More than anything, it is about turning my story inside-out. It is about sharing my story in a way that benefits others.

I used to believe that depression is something that happened to me, but I made a decision to change the focus of my story, and now I think that it happened for me.

Please come along on this journey with me as I take a leap of faith and share some of my most private memories and personal struggles from various stages of my life, with the hope that by making myself vulnerable, lives are saved and families restored.

1 | UNMASKING THE DISEASE

From the outside looking in, it's hard to understand.
From the inside looking out, it's hard to explain.

—Unknown

When I first started writing this book, I made an agreement with myself that this would not be a book about the disease of depression. What would be the point? There are countless books out there sharing their ideas and views on the subject. At the same time, I felt it necessary to confront at least what it is and what it isn't. To this end, it's important to share some initial thoughts and feelings about the disease—from my point of view—before I get into my personal story.

Some people think of depression as a negative emotion that you overcome with the right mindset. Hence, statements borne out of frustration are blurted out:

"What's wrong with you?"

"Can't you just snap out of it?"

"Why can't you just be happy?"

"Just get over it already."

"You only care about yourself."

If only it were that easy, but it's not. Depression is a disease—a mental illness—that negatively affects a person's thinking process and their ability to respond to life conditions with mental and emotional maturity and clarity.

It is a disease that lives inside the brain with a voice that turns you against yourself. It continually sends out signals to tell you that you are useless, stupid, or any other self-defeating thoughts that shred your self-esteem and undermine your will to live.

Although there are many different causes of depression, one thing remains true: the more prolonged depression remains undiagnosed and untreated, the stronger and more destructive it becomes.

For the person suffering from depression, life becomes a state of ever-increasing agony as the disease slowly drains them of all desire to live.

The nature of the disease can also pull the sufferer away from what they need most—compassion, encouragement, love, and support from those who love them—their family and friends—and push them toward isolation. This pulling and pushing happens because the person suffering from depression has difficulty expressing the mental and emotional pain they are experiencing.

As the disease progresses and their condition worsens, the ability to express their internal pain deteriorates. Frustration takes hold and irritability develops. Their behavior is hurtful to family and friends, but they see their loved one struggling and naturally want to understand what is causing it. Unfortunately, the loved one is either too ashamed to talk about how they are feeling, or the disease is far enough along that they are losing awareness of their condition and less capable of expressing their feelings. The level of their frustration and irritability increases and, at times, turns into anger. The loved one's behavior becomes more difficult for their family and friends to handle.

At some point, as family and friends try unsuccessfully to break through to their loved one, it is not uncommon for them to become discouraged. Frustration can take hold. As the loved one continues to sink further into depression, it becomes more likely that their family and friends will move toward a state of desperation. Eventually, losing hope that they will ever be able to help their loved one, they may give up. Once this happens, it is then just a matter of time before an uncontrollable downward spiral begins, as neither the person who is sick nor their family and friends fully understand what is happening—and they all fall into darkness together.

They say that heart disease is the silent killer. You are going about the day, happily enjoying your life, and then suddenly, without a whisper, you're dead. If you have to go, at least there is no period of pain and suffering. I can think of many far worse ways to go, and depression is one of them—perhaps even the worst.

With depression, you are going about the daily drudgery of your existence, and then suddenly, out of nowhere, a wave of despair falls over you. It has happened all too many times before, but you have never been able to get a handle on the trigger for this wave of emotions. It just happens, and all you can do is try to wait it out, desperately hoping it will pass quickly. But then one day, out of nowhere, a wave like no other comes over you. It is a massive, roaring, terrifying tsunami of despair. Helpless, scared, and overwhelmed, you become panic-stricken and completely disoriented. There is no waiting this one out—you are swept away. If heart disease is the silent killer, then depression is the invisible killer.

I did not receive my clinical diagnosis of depression until I was twenty-six years old, and by that point I was in so much denial I brushed off the diagnosis as just being symptomatic of me going through hard times. In reality, depression took its first grip on my life when I was six years old, and over the next more than four decades, I unknowingly progressed through what for me I can best describe as the four stages of depression—leading to the end stage.

STAGE 1: Anxiety: feelings of worry, fear, and helplessness.

STAGE 2: Twisted Thinking: a voice in my mind that sends negative messages to me, clouding my ability to think rationally and positively. Loss of focus and concentration.

STAGE 3: Withdrawal: losing my interest in everybody and everything. Exhaustion: sleeping, waking up and wanting to sleep more. Excessive Irritability. Loneliness.

STAGE 4: Disconnecting: losing touch with life. Detached from family, friends, and the world around me.

END STAGE: Isolation. Hopelessness.

What I believe is the clearest sign of depression would hit me at any time, and without warning over the four stages: feeling sad, often deep sadness, without ever understanding why.

As I progressed through each stage, one building upon another—with all the related turmoil from each stage growing in frequency and intensity—the disease slowly, but ceaselessly, wreaked havoc on my life in subtle and not-so-subtle ways. With all of the emotional ups and downs that I experienced—each a story of its own in my battle with depression—I eventually hit bottom much later in my life.

From the time that I was six years old, as I grew up and moved through adulthood, my mental and emotional struggles never ended. Each second of my life felt like the slow drip-drip of a leaky faucet. Minute-by-minute, hour-by-hour, day-by-day, week-by-week, month-by-month, year-by-year, my challenges progressed and worsened with each passing day. I never fully comprehended what was happening. Then finally, one morning at the age of fifty-one, everything came to a head, and I reached the end stage of depression.

The years of depression had exacted an intolerable toll on me. I had become completely disconnected from the world—present, but absent. I no longer derived any pleasure in life. I was tired all the time, an exhaustion so intense that I could sleep all day and wake up wanting to go right back to sleep. My entire being was frightened to its core. I felt ashamed of what I had been reduced to—a lifeless burden to my wife and son. Alone, scared, helpless, worthless, ashamed, and finally—hopeless.

2 | ESCAPE THROUGH KLONOPIN

I don't want to see anyone. I lie in the bedroom with the
curtains drawn and nothingness washing over me like a
sluggish wave. Whatever is happening to me is my own fault.
I have done something wrong, something so huge I can't even
see it, something that's drowning me. I am inadequate and
stupid, without worth. I might as well be dead.

—Margaret Atwood

DEPRESSION | END STAGE

It is October of 2014. I am now fifty-one years old. I have come to the realization that I am an enormous burden to my family.

I no longer have any energy because my depression has robbed my body, mind, and spirit of its life. Somehow, I gather the strength to get out of bed.

Another day is about to begin in a job where my performance has turned out to be a colossal disappointment. I had been hired about six months prior with much enthusiasm about the contribution I was going to make to the firm in a high-level position. But early on, the pressure of not being able to keep up with the pace of work quickly began to take hold. I do not fit into the firm's culture, performing far below expectations, and with each passing day, I feel as though I am being treated with the same disdain as a leper. It has all become too overwhelming for me, and I feel like I have nothing left to give.

Perhaps, if I had not been fighting depression for so many years, the day would take a different course. Maybe, if I had not stayed in an industry that I hated for the past twenty-seven years, this day would turn out to be an exciting and happy one. Perhaps if I had not been under the care of an incompetent psychiatrist for the past eight years, I would have never even arrived at this crisis point. She threw every medication in the book at me in a futile attempt to alleviate my symptoms—ultimately recommending electroconvulsive therapy (ECT) because, well, why not? I felt like her lab rat. Maybe, just maybe, if I had a person in my life who I could trust enough to confide in about how desperate I have become, this day would have turned out differently. There is someone—my wife, but the disease has taken over not only my mind, but also our relationship, and I'm just too sick to do anything about it.

I use every ounce of energy I have left to get up. Then, I slowly walk toward the bathroom. Opening my medicine cabinet, I reach for the bottle of Klonopin, a drug used to treat panic disorders and anxiety. Other than sleep, this drug has become the only thing that gives me any relief whatsoever from the all-consuming anxiety and despair that has taken hold of me. But without Klonopin, sleep has become almost impossible. I twist the bottle open, turn it over, and let a stream of pills fall into my hand. Without hesitation, I tilt my head back, and within an instant, my open palm is against my mouth. The pills fall in, and I swallow all of them. It is not hard.

I have reached a state of total desperation. I need a way to numb my feelings, to help settle me down and get through another day. Taking all these pills is not a voluntary or intentional act. Depression was running its ordinary course. My brain was totally diseased, and my thoughts and actions were no longer my own. Reality had all but vanished, and physical movements were now the result of a mind that had just completed an unhealthy metamorphosis. In short—all rationale was gone. I was no longer myself. The act of swallowing more Klonopin than is considered safe is the result of a depressed brain that re-animated to conclude the end stage of depression.

Somehow, I make it to the office. I go to my desk, and within an hour I collapse. Emergency personnel take me out on a stretcher, roll me into the ambulance, and proceed to bombard me with questions—anything to keep me awake.

Hours later, my eyes slowly open as I lay on a bed in an emergency room at Porter Hospital in Denver. I see two security guards—at least I think there were two—standing at the entrance to the hospital room. I feel a tap on my shoulder, and turn my head to see a doctor sitting next to me. He is a psychiatrist. My life has changed forever, and I have no idea how it happened.

As I look back upon this day, I see it as an end and a beginning to my long and uncertain journey toward healing.

3 | FORGOTTEN JOY

If children feel safe, they can take risks, ask questions,
make mistakes, learn to trust, share their feelings, and grow.

—Alfie Kohn

For most people, happiness and joy are emotions that are naturally easy to experience. Happiness is in the mind and comes from enjoying magical moments in time. Joy is in the spirit. It is a light, uplifting feeling that comes from within one's heart and mind. Happiness and joy are not easy for me to feel and connect with. I must have been between four and five years old when I last experienced the feeling of pure, untethered, child-like joy. It would happen at the end of each day of nursery school.

It is 1967. Another day of nursery school just ended, and all of us kids get to spend the last part of the day on the playground doing whatever we want while waiting for our parents. I love the playground. Going down the slide and falling into the sand is a big favorite of mine, along with the merry-go-round.

Each time I hop on the merry-go-round, I make it go as fast as I can and then hold on for dear life. The breeze feels so good across my face and in my hair. It makes me feel alive. As the merry-go-round slows down and comes to a stop, I stumble off, feeling dizzy, happy, and carefree. So much fun!

But my favorite thing to do on the playground is to climb on the jungle gym. I love the challenge, and I always manage to work my way to the top of the metal structure. Before I begin my ascent, I look up at the tippy-top. It never seems like it is that far up, but without fail, once I make it to the top and then get ready to come down, the view is very different up there. From that vantage point, the ground suddenly looks like it is twenty feet below. Gulp. But then I carefully work my way down. It's always a bit scary looking down from the peak, but that's what makes the whole round-trip so much fun—quite the daily adventure for me.

The most significant part of playing on the jungle gym at the end of each day is that, like clockwork, I see my mom walking toward the playground from the parking lot. As soon as I see her, no matter how high I am, my only thought is how fast I can get down. Forget about ever feeling scared—I jump off that jungle gym with reckless abandon and run as fast as I can toward her open arms. My mom is always happy and smiling as she kneels and waits for me to make the final leap into her arms, at which point she swoops me up off the ground and hugs me tightly like she is never going to let me go. I wrap my arms around her neck and rest my head on her shoulder. And then, for a moment in time, I feel nothing but bliss. My whole being fills with something far more profound and stronger than happiness. What that feeling is, I cannot describe. Who cares? I just never want it to go away!

I have countless memories from childhood, yet none are even remotely as clear as those moments of joy at the end of nursery school. As I look back now, I realize that I took those feelings for granted, and I had no idea how foreign they would become to me later in my life.

As I struggle to understand how I got from the highest point of natural bliss at age four to total despair at age fifty-one, I have asked myself countless numbers of questions. One of them is: *was* there any particular reason why the memory of joy in nursery school held such a singularly vivid presence in my mind for so many years? I believe that the memory became a lasting source of hope.

At some point, in my earliest years of childhood, the disease, commonly referred to as "depression," under the heading of "mental illness," likely presented itself and started on its steady path of destruction. Over the years, in the midst of the attack, my mind clung to that memory of joy. And, given the events that were about to unfold, I can now understand why.

4 | RUSTY BRAIN

*In a way, bullying is an ordinary evil. It's hugely
prevalent, all too often ignored—and being ignored,
it is therefore condoned.*

—Trudie Styler

DEPRESSION STAGE ONE | ANXIETY

My first day of kindergarten is about to begin. I feel happy because my mom is walking me down the hallway toward the classroom. Like any other five-year-old, I have no idea of the change that is about to take place in my life. If kindergarten is anything like nursery school, another day of fun is on the way, and my mom is holding my hand and guiding me toward it. I feel safe and at peace because she is with me, and I see her warm, caring smile.

Then, all of a sudden, when we arrive at the classroom, everything feels different. My new teacher opens the door to welcome me in, and all I can focus on are the rows of desks with many kids already sitting in them. This setting feels very different than nursery school. I am surprised and unsettled, and it doesn't seem natural to me. My mind scrambles as I think back on my memories of nursery school.

When I went to nursery school, there were never rows of desks. The rooms were filled with exciting things to do and places to explore. There were toys, coloring books, an arts and crafts table, and big playsets where we all could climb. Who wouldn't want to walk into that setting?

I know nursery school is a place to learn, but it never felt sterile and formal like this kindergarten classroom. I couldn't wait to go to nursery school every day. It was a welcoming, exciting environment, and I naturally gravitated toward it. Every day was full of exploration and discovery.

But now, here I am at the entrance of a very different world, and it makes me uneasy. As my kindergarten teacher reaches out to welcome me, I step back and hold onto my mom's hand tightly. She immediately knows I don't want to go into the classroom and kneels to reassure me. But it is not enough to make me feel comfortable about leaving her to go into this classroom. I want to be safe in her arms, just like nursery school.

Tears start falling down my face as she continues to encourage me to go with my new teacher into the classroom. I am becoming increasingly nervous and scared as she continues to reassure me to let go of her and walk into the classroom. But the tears start coming down harder and faster as my anxiety level swells. Nothing, however, would change the inevitable. My mom, holding my hand, leads me into the classroom. The teacher takes my hand and tries to calm me down. Through the tears, I watch as my mom walks away. I understand that she has to leave, but I am just not prepared for it. This situation is new, and my uncertainty and anxiousness are like nothing I have ever felt.

I completed my first year of kindergarten—well, what turned out to be my first year. Apparently, I wasn't learning. I couldn't read, and my parents were concerned about potential diminished mental capabilities, more accurately referred to in those days as mental retardation. They decided to hold me back. All that I knew at the time was that my friends were now in first grade, and I wasn't. I was confused.

It is the first day of my second year of kindergarten, and I am hesitant to enter the classroom. Starting over again is now a reality. By mid-morning, I am beginning to settle in and adapt to my circumstances. But the initial sense of calm rapidly disappears.

Before I even begin to make new friends, I run into my buddies from last year, and I quickly learn that they no longer want to be friends with me. I don't understand why, but I start to feel anxiety and fear as the torment begins. First comes the teasing. A couple of their favorite things to say as they laugh at me are:

"Bobby failed Juice and Cookies."

"Rusty brain!" A reference to my red hair.

They are having fun. I am devastated. Why has everything changed? It makes no sense, but this is just the beginning.

As the first weeks of my second attempt at kindergarten unfold, the teasing turns to hitting and kicking. Monday recess is when it first happens. I am at the top of the playground slide, getting ready to come down. I love the slide. But everything changes. I zoom down to the bottom of the slide just like I always do. This time, my former friends surround me. They start kicking me. I curl up and try to protect myself.

Some of them start punching me while the kicking continues.

I am lying on the ground, curled up as tightly as I can, with my eyes closed and tears streaming down my face, waiting for it to end. When it finally stops, I don't move for some time. How long, I don't know. I just hoped that when I opened my eyes, the boys would no longer be there.

I have no idea why, but none of the teachers see what is going on. They are supposed to protect us during recess, but they are not protecting me. I used to love recess, but after this moment, now I hate it. I hate walking down the halls inside. I hate school.

No surprise, I do what any six-year-old does when they want to avoid school. I wake up every Monday morning with a stomach ache. It's worth a shot, but it never works. Real or not, a stomach ache doesn't get me out of it. Mom drags me out of bed, telling me I cannot miss school.

I wish my mom would ask me why I always want to avoid going to school on Mondays and why I'm so unhappy with school, but she never asks. So off I go, feeling unsafe and on my own, walking down the halls, never knowing when I am going to get teased again.

Looking back at what it felt like to go to school every day that second year of kindergarten, I see a frightened little boy entering his war zone and never understanding why he did not even feel safe at home, let alone at school. At that young age, I began to experience what it is like to feel helpless, and that feeling carried into my adult life.

5 | SILENCE IS NOT A COPING SKILL

Every day, in 100 small ways, our children ask,
'Do you hear me? Do you see me? Do I matter?'
Their behavior often reflects our response.

—L.R. Knost

Over the next couple of years, the teasing slowly diminished as my classmates from my first year of kindergarten moved on to other things. The constant feeling of being unsafe and frightened was fading, and I made two great friends—Eddie and Frank—who added some degree of normalcy to my life. I have great memories of doing all kinds of fun things with Eddie and Frank. We played basketball, tag football, roller hockey (in Eddie's driveway), wiffle ball in a local park, stickball in the street, board games, video games, miniature golf, sleigh riding, and the list goes on—pretty much anything you can think of that great buddies would do together growing up.

While it never occurred to me at the time, decades later, I have come to realize that Eddie and Frank were the only people in school that I consistently felt safe and happy to be around. They were both fun, kind, and genuine. And most importantly, I knew they always had my back.

While it felt like I was walking straight into a battlefield every day I went to school, there was some relief knowing that I had two buddies on my side who liked and understood me. Without ever knowing it, Eddie and Frank helped me to survive. Though much time has passed since I last spoke with either of them, having all gone our separate ways, I am forever thankful for their friendship.

As great as it was to have two solid friends that I could always rely on, it did not change the fact that I continued to hate going to school. Learning was difficult for me and, while I tried as hard as I could to understand and keep up with the work, I found myself falling more and more behind each day. Nobody could understand why I had so much trouble learning, and my parents began to worry that I had a learning disability. They had me go through a series of tests to evaluate my mental capabilities, but none showed any signs of learning problems.

So, with the knowledge that my capacity to learn was not an issue, why I was unable to keep pace with my classmates remained a mystery. My mom made every effort to help me. She worked with the school to assign me a tutor. This person worked with me to try and help close the gap between being able to learn and, at the same time, keep up with the other students.

I liked working with my tutor. She was kind and patient as she guided me through different exercises to help me speed up my learning process. It was always a relief to get out of class and work with her.

Unfortunately, the tutoring was not improving the speed at which I could learn. But it did provide a much-needed break from the mounting stress I felt trying to keep up with the other students.

While these learning difficulties were taking a toll on me, every day after school my friend Mitch and I began playing a lot of basketball together. Mitch lived in the neighborhood, and we played at his house. We both enjoyed the time shooting hoops, and our friendship grew. The sport helped get my mind off of the stress from school that was continuously overwhelming me. I had a natural talent for the game, and Mitch, being two years my senior, took on the role of coaching me.

Those basketball sessions were fun and a welcome relief from my troubles at school. As time went by, however, the fun steadily diminished. Intramural school league play began in third grade. Having practiced with Mitch well before any of the other kids started participating in the school competitions, I immediately stood out as a top performer.

At first, it felt great being way better than my classmates and the other players from different schools that we competed against. It was the opposite of how it felt always being behind my classmates academically. Mitch was an extremely competitive person, and while that was a positive influence in some ways—he helped me to become a better player—it also had a critical downside. The constant pressure was gradually replacing the fun and enjoyment of playing with him because I had to keep up with his competitive nature and the ever-increasing intensity of his coaching.

In league play, I remained a top player, but as other kids played more and more, the performance gap I had when league play began was decreasing. The sport that had provided me with a needed outlet from my learning frustrations had become another pressure in my life.

Maintaining my initial status as one of the best players in the league, combined with the increasing demand Mitch was placing on me was proving to be too much. By the final couple of games of the season, I found myself not wanting to play anymore.

The pressure to be the best was very stressful to me, and I would tell my dad that my ankle hurt in the hopes that he would tell me to stay off the court until he could get it checked by a doctor. It was feeling like my second year of kindergarten all over again, but under different circumstances. I had developed strong anxiety about meeting the expectations of being a standout player. My dad was one of two coaches leading our team. He was focused on preparing for the game and did not take my complaint seriously. I did not bring it up again.

I had already learned during the days of my repeat year of kindergarten that any attempt to avoid a situation I did not want to get into would be met with anger and dismissiveness—no interest in going down that dead-end again. So, I was left with a growing sense of helplessness. My way of trying to get through situations that heightened my anxiety level was to fight through them in silence. As it turns out, this was not an optimal life strategy.

6 | DOUBLE TROUBLE

There is a plan and a purpose, a value to every life,
no matter what its location, age, gender or disability.
—Sharron Angle

Imagine my frustration. I was just a kid, and all I wanted to do was fit in, have friends like everyone else, and enjoy school and sports. Not so fast. What was simple for all the other kids was a never-ending struggle for me, and the hardest part was not knowing why. In the back of my mind, I was always asking myself the same questions:

Why me?

Why is it so hard for me to do my schoolwork?

What's wrong with me?

I finally got my answer in fourth grade. I was diagnosed with dyslexia and Duane Syndrome. Either one of these by themselves would cause a significant headwind in terms of learning and keeping up with classmates, but combine them, and the headwind is massive.

The vast majority of people have heard of dyslexia and typically associate it with reversing numbers and letters. Dyslexia, however, is more than that. It impacts one's entire capability to process information, creating major hurdles to learn at the same pace as those without it.

When I was diagnosed with dyslexia, I had no understanding of what it was or the magnitude of the problems it was creating for me. The word itself confused me. As far as I was concerned, you could call it whatever you wanted, the impact on me was still the same: I had feelings of frustration and helplessness, stress and anxiety. It took forever for me to learn, and the process was draining. I felt like I had a scrambled brain. I even pronounced many words in a strange way. Instead of "music," I used to say: "usmic." My self-esteem took a major hit.

Unlike dyslexia, almost nobody has ever heard of Duane Syndrome. It is not surprising, as only approximately one-tenth of one percent of the world's population has it. Duane Syndrome is a disorder that affects eye movement. It is characterized by limitation of the inward or outward horizontal motion of the eye. In my case, it was the right eye that was affected. It would not move outward. So, when I started to read a line in a book, as I scanned from left to right, only my left eye moved across the page. My right eye could not. The result: I would see double. It was extremely frustrating and demoralizing.

Eventually I learned to turn my head from left to right instead. It eliminated the double vision but created a different problem. When I reached the end of a line of reading and then turned my head left to move down to the beginning of the next line of the page, I would often skip to the line below it by mistake. Talk about frustration. The solution to that problem? A ruler. I would place it underneath the first line on the page, read it, and then move the ruler down to the next line, read that one and then move the ruler down again, and so on and so forth. Needless to say,

I was never going to win a speed-reading contest. Eventually, I tossed out the ruler and just tried to stay focused on not skipping lines. Of course, I continued to skip lines, and still do to this day.

I remember my diagnoses of dyslexia and Duane Syndrome being a significant relief for my parents. They finally had an explanation for why I was struggling so much in school. No one wants their child to have to deal with the challenges of a disability, but at least they were now able to make sense of all my struggles in school.

The learning headwinds and energy drain that resulted from the combination of dyslexia and Duane Syndrome became another source of fuel for my depression.

7 | CHAOS

When you're depressed, you don't control your thoughts, your
thoughts control you. I wish people understood that.

—Unknown

DEPRESSION STAGE TWO |
TWISTED THINKING

While I had my share of problems in elementary school, by fifth grade, I had reached a reasonable level of comfort. I had two great friends and had become aware of the challenges that were making learning more difficult for me. The depression was there, and while problematic, it had yet to fully and dramatically impair my life.

As the summer between elementary and middle school wound down, my anxiety level mounted. I had always been sad as summer came to an end, knowing another year of school was coming, but this time the feeling was different. I was about to step into the unknown, and it was frightening. The middle school was much larger. Kids from the surrounding schools would all be converging, and I knew the academic demands would increase. The anticipation of all this change was not a good mix for me. The one thing that helped temper my anxiety was that my two buddies would be there, and we would likely be in a few classes together, as requested by my mom. Still, the thought of this significant change weighed heavily on me.

I remember feeling lost on the first day of middle school. I entered homeroom—which in and of itself was a new experience for me—and walked into what seemed like a chaotic environment: all new faces, lots of loud chatter, and a colder classroom atmosphere. I have little doubt that many students had their worries about beginning middle school, but they all seemed to have a level of excitement that went with it as they met each other that first morning. I had none.

As I sat in homeroom, my mind became flooded with negative thoughts. While I do not pretend to recall precisely what they were, I do remember the general thoughts racing through my brain:

You are in way over your head, Bobby.

Why can't you try to interact with the other students?

Why can't you just calm down and get a grip on yourself?

These negative thoughts were only making things worse. For some reason, I just couldn't keep everything in perspective. My anxiety level spiked. I started to feel completely overwhelmed. And then, out of nowhere, a wave of sadness hit me. I didn't want to be in that classroom. I didn't want to be in that school. But there was no way out. The situation was hopeless—at least that was what my mind had convinced me.

As the first few weeks of middle school unfolded, my anxiety lessened somewhat but remained at an elevated level compared to my last year of elementary school. As tricky as elementary school had been for me, in middle school, I faced new challenges above and beyond my learning difficulties.

The first new challenge was that the ringing of a bell separated classes, and then everybody had only a few minutes—I think it was five—to get to their next classroom. This hectic pace was overwhelming. I learned something new about myself as a result of this regimented schedule: I had no sense of direction.

The middle school building was massive compared to my elementary school. Navigating the hallways and stairs to get to the next class on time was no easy task for me and was extremely stressful. That feeling of being overwhelmed returned each time the bell rang. It drained me both mentally and physically, and no doubt aggravated my stress and anxiety, fueling the advance of my depression. Having dyslexia and Duane Syndrome probably contributed to my challenges with navigation.

My next big challenge was lunchtime. When I was in elementary school, my mom used to pick me up at school for lunch and then take me back. That was great. I have happy memories from those times. But there was a cafeteria in middle school, and lunchtime was spent there every day.

For any ordinary kid, lunch in the cafeteria is a fun and happy time to chat and play with friends. And that is the way it started out for me. But then, one day, everything changed. It was in the cafeteria within the first few months of school when things went south. I was sitting at a table with Eddie, Frank, and a few other students. We were having a good time talking and eating our lunch together, but then, out of nowhere, we were interrupted by a person we had never met before. He looked like he was a seventh grader and was accompanied by a few of his friends. He started to give us a hard time, just looking to intimidate us, for whatever reason, I didn't know.

I did what seemed like the right thing at that moment. I stood up and told him to back off. Looking back, I think a part of my knee-jerk reaction to stand up to him was from my experience of having been beaten up during my second round of kindergarten. I think at that moment after the seventh grader started bullying us, the only thing that came into my mind was that I didn't want to repeat that experience. While it might have been the right thing to do, it turned out to be a big, big mistake. He came toward me and essentially said I was going to regret saying that. His friends—really, his middle school gang members—were right there with him and were as happy as could be. He sounded very serious, and I had a bad feeling about what was to come. My moment of strength was quickly replaced by fear. Instead of striking back, I folded.

I soon learned that he had a reputation of being a dangerous person—more than just your average bully—and I was his new target. It was the last thing I needed. There I was again, on high alert wherever I went—inside the building and out—all day, every day.

One day, I was hurrying down a hallway trying to get to my next class. As I was rushing to get there in time, I turned my head for a moment and didn't realize a person was coming toward me from the opposite direction. I ran straight into him—and just my luck, yes, it was the bully. He went berserk. I just froze. I caught a break because other guys in the hallway came over to get in-between us. They had to restrain him because he was so intent in his desire to beat me up. He slowly settled down as I turned away to go in the opposite direction. That event sealed my fate. Why did he have to be the one person that I ran into by mistake? I knew things were about to get worse, and they did.

From that point forward, every time I saw him in the hallway, he would torment me with threats about beating me up and giving me the sense that it could be worse. It took a psychological toll on me, and I didn't know what to do. The obvious thing to do would have been to tell my parents and see if they could help me with this situation, but the thought never really crossed my mind. That kind of thinking had already passed, and so I just continued down the path of slow but steady withdrawal—just part of the progressive nature of depression.

8 | THE INVISIBLE MAN

You wear a mask for so long,
you forget who you were beneath it.
—Alan Moore

HALLOWEEN SCARE

One day after school, about a week before Halloween, I was outside—I think at the bike rack, unlocking my bike chain to ride home. As I was doing this, I looked up and saw the bully approach. As he walked toward me, he said he was going to bring a knife with him on Halloween and come after me. Whether or not he was serious at the time, I will never be sure, but he did have a menacing, intimidating look on his face, and he hated me for pushing back at him that day in the cafeteria. I became worried and frightened.

That evening after dinner, I was so overwhelmed by fear because of what had happened at the bike rack after school, I went to talk to my parents. The severity of the anxiety I had was so intense that I set aside my default behavior of fighting through difficult situations on my own. There was nothing else I could do. I took the threat seriously, and if ever there was a time for my parents to get involved and help me, this was it.

When I told them what had happened and the person who made the threat, I remember them being very concerned. We discussed the situation for quite some time. In the end, they concluded that it was just another kid who was trying to make me afraid of him, but these kinds of things happened in middle school. There was no reason to overreact. I think they believed I needed to be able to handle the situation on my own, that it would make me a stronger person, but I couldn't.

I remember that being a pivotal moment for me growing up. In my mind, whether right or wrong, I relinquished any hope of ever feeling protected. Instead of finding my strength as I believe my parents had hoped, I learned how to feel powerless—a feeling that altered the course of my life.

When Halloween finally arrived, I was extremely nervous. I did not know what danger awaited. Would he be looking for me? If he did, would he come after me with a knife as promised? Would a bunch of his friends be with him, and what would they do to make things worse? I didn't know what to do that night, but then I had an idea. I decided to make my costume so incredible that nobody would ever know who I was. It seemed sensible at the time. I had so much fear that I did not miss a detail as I prepared to make myself impossible to know. I remember even taking a permanent ink marker and covering my name on each of my sneakers. How I ever thought he would find me by seeing my name on the top front of each of my sneakers, I don't know. But that was the level of fear he had instilled in me.

My friends and I had made plans to meet at Eddie's house and then go trick-or-treating together. When I got to Eddie's house, his mom answered the door. She stared at me for a few seconds with a look of puzzlement on her face. She knew Eddie had invited everybody to meet at his house around this time and was expecting one of us to be on the other side of the door. But she didn't recognize me. Then, I looked at her through my mask and said, "hello, Mrs. Zimmerman." She looked bewildered, but must have recognized my voice just enough to reply, "Bobby, is that you?" I said, "yes, Mrs. Zimmerman, this is me." She gave a sigh of relief and let me in.

Eddie had just come to the door as his mother let me in. He was very happy and shouted out, "Strausssyyy!" before signaling for me to follow him back to the kitchen. Everybody was already chatting away, laughing, and having a great time. I joined in the fun. We were all excited to be together and ready to go out and see how much candy we could get. I was relieved that Eddie's mom didn't know who I was. Mission accomplished. I was incognito.

As it turned out, I never ended up running into the bully that night and ended up having a total blast. It also turned out to be our last Halloween of trick-or-treating together. We were reaching the age when it would become awkward going door-to-door dressed in a costume and saying, "Trick-or-Treat." But I loved that night, oh how I loved that night. And the best part was how my ability to hide my true identity resulted in feelings of increased safety and less fear.

Now, I look back with my adult eyes and realize how ridiculous my mindset was that night. Of course, the costume did not make me any safer. The bully would have seen our whole group and known I was with them. And covering my name on my sneakers with permanent ink—what a worthless waste of time. Talk about being consumed by fear—but it all made sense back then.

That night, without realizing it until years later—decades too late—I convinced myself that hiding my identity would make me safe, and from that point forward I created a mask—a false identity that carried into my adulthood. It was a foolish and catastrophic takeaway. All it ended up doing was putting me on a path of feeling an ever-increasing sense of loneliness; at the same time, it drained me of all my energy.

I survived middle school, but not without one additional lasting effect: from that point in my life forward, every day and everywhere I have gone, for my self-protection, I have walked through life in a hypervigilant state of mind.

9 | THE GENERAL

Powerlessness is an excruciating pain;
it is torture insurmountable.
—Richelle E. Goodrich

Over my three years in middle school, Mitch and I spent an increasing amount of time with each other. We continued to play basketball together and started having fun doing other athletic activities. We would toss the football back and forth. We invented a way to play one-on-one baseball. We raced bikes and competed in swimming races with each other. There were golf days, tennis matches, and bowling competitions. In short, we did everything together, and it was a lot of fun—for a while.

The intensity that Mitch had when he started coaching me in basketball ramped up and worked its way into everything. Over time he started to become controlling and dominating. I was already feeling pretty beaten down as it was, so there wasn't much fight left in me. It seemed as if Mitch had a sense of just how weak I had become and took full advantage of it. I quickly learned that he was the boss, and I was to follow his lead. Mitch would decide what we were going to play, and when. I either went along with him or endured his wrath. Before I knew it, there was no turning back.

The baseball game that we played involved trying to hit a tennis ball against a wall. The wall was the back of his parents' house. It would boomerang back over us and beyond a fence behind us. It was like trying to hit home runs. Whoever hit the most would win. There was more to it, but that was the basic premise. Every once in a while, one of us would hit the tennis ball so high that instead of bouncing back off the wall, it would fly straight over the house. Mitch would send me off to go get it, which, of course, I did.

Sometimes, instead of going over the house, the ball would bounce off the roof and roll back into the gutter above us. It was not uncommon for all of the tennis balls we had to get stuck in the gutters. At that point, either we stopped playing until we could get additional tennis balls, or somebody would have to go up on the roof and retrieve them, and it wasn't Mitch.

His parents owned a big house, and the roof was about thirty feet from the ground. Recovering the tennis balls required going inside the house and up to the attic. Then, there was one window that gave access to the portion of the roof where the gutter with the tennis balls was. The slope of the roof was steep, so trying to get from the window to the gutter was dangerous. Walking was not an option. Instead, you had to carefully slide your way down using your hands and feet as breaks. If it had rained recently, it could get slippery, so the slide down to the gutter had to be very deliberate.

Neither of us wanted to stop playing, but the idea of going up on the roof to recover the tennis balls was enough to give us both pause. Our love of the game was put to the test—one of us would have to step up to the plate. But who would it be? I could see the coin toss in Mitch's head. It was a heads-he-wins-tails-I-lose situation. Mitch gave the command and off I went to get the tennis balls. It scared the living daylights out of me every time. I remember slowly working my way toward the gutter while trying not to look down. Very hard to do. And, whenever I did look down, there was Mitch, happy as could be. All smiles.

At the time, I would try to laugh it off and convince myself it wasn't that big of a deal, which is precisely the message I got from Mitch. But there was really nothing funny about it. It was foolish, dangerous, and stupid, and Mitch knew it. That's why I was on the roof, and he was watching from the ground.

I had a love-hate relationship with Mitch. I loved what we did together, but I hated how he treated me because it fueled my insecurities. If depression had an army of soldiers, Mitch would be the general.

As Mitch and I spent more time together, I took greater notice of his personality. I started to see an angry, explosive side to him. His emotional eruptions were never predictable. I learned quickly to do whatever Mitch said or run the risk of being subject to one of them. I never knew when he was going to become furious about something, and it made being around him extremely nerve-racking.

Mitch's natural inclination to intimidate me slowly and systematically caused harm to my state of mind. I never realized the massive impact Mitch had on fueling my depression until it was too late. How could I? Growing up, we were the best of friends—at least I thought so. I now clearly understand that this was never the case. I was his friend, but Mitch was never mine.

In everything we did together, it seemed as though Mitch took great pleasure in intimidating, harassing, and demeaning me. It was his nature to bully me into doing whatever he wanted. Sometimes it would be the threat of physical harm, and other times it would be a psychological attack. Sometimes both. He seemed to derive great pleasure in demeaning and embarrassing me and frightening me with his size and strength.

Anytime I dared to disagree with Mitch, no matter how trivial the topic, I remember the consequences—a rage would well up inside of him as he stuck his chest out, cocked his arm back and raised his fist at me; all the while his eyes bulged out of his sockets as he glared down at me. Then, Mitch would start moving toward me. He didn't run; it was more of an aggressive, stalking walk that gained momentum as he drew closer. It was intimidating by design. Everything Mitch did was planned and purposeful.

As he came closer and closer, he would be yelling and telling me: "Bobby, you don't know what the fuck you're talking about!"

His voice was filled with fury—how dare I disagree with him? My heart would pound as he came toward me. I felt scared and beaten down. One more word and Mitch was going to beat the living daylights out of me. It was a hopeless situation. There was no way out except to take back my opinion, shut up, and wait for him to calm down.

What types of disagreements am I referring to? They were really important things like who was the best basketball player of all time, or who was the better of two top major league baseball teams.

Bullies do not prey on strong people. Mitch knew my weaknesses. Instead of being a solid friend and helping me to become stronger and more confident, he preyed upon my vulnerabilities. As with all bullies, doing so made him feel better at my expense. He built up his self-esteem by putting me down.

And Mitch had energy like no other person I have ever met. He never stopped, always in a constant state of agitation. Being with him was stressful and taxing. It was like standing next to a volcano that was forever bubbling at the surface, ready to erupt in rage at any second. Not somebody that anyone would want to go near. Yet there I was, together with him most of the time.

Mitch's verbal attacks and sudden outbursts of anger steadily took their toll on me. Out of fear of retribution, I became extremely careful about what I said and how I said it. Containing my natural desire to stick-up for myself was tiring, but necessary, and with each incident of being subject to his abusive behavior, my resilience became weaker and weaker. At some point, exactly when I am not sure, it was gone.

10 | FADING HOPES AND FLYING CAPS

*And I knew it was bad when I woke up in
the mornings and the only thing I looked
forward to was going back to bed.*

—Unknown

DEPRESSION STAGE 3 | WITHDRAWAL

The start of summer provided a much-needed break from what was an extremely turbulent and unsettling three years in middle school. I was now being removed, through the natural course of life, from what had become an unbearable situation. I didn't want to think about school. I had a window of relief, and I never wanted to let go of it. But the thoughts of beginning high school inevitably started. I tried as hard as I possibly could to hold onto the hope that high school would be better. Predictably, the hope did not last long.

As the last days of summer closed in, my lingering sense of hope was dimming. I had learned to hate school; it was irreversible. Sunday nights were a horror show—the start of a new week meant I was going back into the war zone. The next five days, I would be in a state of hypervigilance as I walked the hallways to and from classes. I couldn't get past these feelings. They had become a part of me.

After a summer of being away, the eve of a new school year brought massive anxiety. Yes, middle school was over, but school was still school. There was no way around it. Objectively, I had reason to be hopeful, but somewhere along the line, fear and anxiety had become dominant forces in my life. Putting middle school behind me was not about to change that.

Surprisingly, early on in high school, it seemed as though the change was going to put me on a healthier path. I had made new friendships in middle school that followed me into high school, and I was having lots of great times with them. One of those friends was Tommy. He was a real character, and I say this with a happy heart. He was also about as sarcastic as they come but in a spirited, happy-go-lucky way. Eddie and Frank continued to be rock-solid friends. Together along with a handful of buddies, I was able to experience some much-needed genuinely fun times.

One of my best memories of this period in my life was during wintertime. When the snow fell, sledding was automatic. But it was much more than just riding down hills. We all got together in the late afternoon, meeting at Eddie's house. He lived right near a private country club with a big hill that was perfect for sledding. If my memory serves me correctly, the hill was partly on the golf course. Since it was a private club, we were not supposed to be on the grounds, but this was just a minor detail that we conveniently ignored.

Without a second of hesitation, we would hop the fence, help each other get our sleds over it, and off we went. We ran through the snow as fast as we could to make our way to the top of the hill. Then, we threw the sleds onto the snow-covered ground, and it was off to the races.

On the way down, as our sleds gained speed, we would often try to steer toward one another—a tactic designed to knock a competitor off and out of the race. It was a great feeling if you could execute this tactic; the ultimate high was if you did it so well that you got to see your buddy flying off of his sled and tumbling through the snow as you passed him. For those that focused on steering clear of these downhill battles and did so successfully, they would be going at breakneck speed toward the bottom of the hill where, staring them right in the face was the very same fence that we all just hopped over as if it didn't even exist. Victory would often come at a price.

Every once in a while, the snow turned to ice, and life was never better. The ride down became much faster and the ability to control the sled far more difficult. The danger of spinning out of control and being thrown from your sled made the race all the more fun. The probability of slamming right into a big tree trunk was ever-present.

We would race down that hill well into the night. I can remember those moments so well. Sledding in the winter with great friends got me close to a sense of joy. Pretty incredible given what was growing inside of me. To this day, the happiness associated with these memories is powerful, but they also bring with them a sense of sadness. The happiness of this magnitude, even bordering on joy, became increasingly difficult to experience.

∞

Throughout high school, depression was becoming the dominant force in my mind and slowly but surely stealing my life. Each passing year pulled me farther and farther away from connectedness to the world.

I didn't fully understand what was happening to me, but I was aware of my increasing lack of desire to be with anyone.

Sleep was my refuge. It was the only thing that provided relief from the relentless internal suffering. It did not help, however, to renew my energy. Quite the opposite—it was an escape from the world, and the more I got, the more I wanted. I craved anything I could do to separate myself from all that was around me. It was a natural, systematic withdrawal. The depression was taking grasp of me. Sleep was never going to stop it.

As high school came to a close, it was time for graduation day. At that point, I had become completely withdrawn. Things that had given me pleasure in the past no longer did so. I had all but lost interest in everything.

So, there I was, sitting in a sea of folding chairs outside on the school grounds. We were a relatively large school, so there were many of us. It was a sunny day, and there was a lot of excitement. There was a sense of pride all around. After all, this day was a significant achievement and marked a milestone in our lives.

Friends and family were there to share in the hopes and dreams of a bright future ahead for all the graduates. I could feel it and see it all around me. I could see my mom and dad in the crowd as I walked up to the podium and received my diploma. They were beaming. As the ceremony came to a close, we were pronounced the graduating class of 1982. I remember hats flying up toward the sky as a roar of excitement about the future filled the air. I looked around and felt silence amidst the joy. Everything seemed like it was happening in slow motion, and I was watching it, unaware of the significance of it all. But I just wanted to leave. For me, it was one more part of life I had to get through. Whatever else lay ahead, I could not have cared less.

11 | GRADUATING CEREMONY—WHERE ARE MY FRIENDS?

I am in that temper that if I were underwater
I would scarcely kick to come to the top.
—John Keats

DEPRESSION STAGE FOUR | DISCONNECTING

I was interested in journalism and visited several well-respected schools that had excellent journalism programs. After much consideration, I ultimately decided to go to a school in upstate New York. Skidmore College was in Saratoga Springs, a beautiful town that was well known for being the home of one of the greatest thoroughbred tracks in the United States. It was a historic track, and unlike so many others, Saratoga still had the nostalgic feel of a place where thoroughbred racing was still the sport of kings. That was not the reason I decided to go there, but having gone to the track a few times, it was why I had some familiarity with the area.

The primary reason I went to Skidmore College was that it was well known for its top-flight journalism program. Scratch that. It didn't have one. Shocking, I know. The truth is, by the time I got out of high school, I had lost interest in so much of life. Going to college was just another thing I was supposed to do. I didn't have the grades to get into an Ivy League school, nor the desire. I wasn't excited about the future. I never put any serious thought into what that future might look like for me.

Skidmore was a small school, which was essential to me because I wanted to feel safe and free from the intimidation of a larger school. It was located in a beautiful little town. The college was far enough from my family that I could experience life on my own, but close enough that I could drive back for a long weekend if I wanted to. My friend Tommy was already enrolled, and I liked the idea of having a friend right from the start. And that was about it. Off I went.

I ended up spending one year at Skidmore. Drinking took up a large portion of my time. The academics bored me, and I was just going through the motions. It was not the right spot for me. The one positive takeaway from this experience was that it made me realize that I really did have an interest in journalism and needed to move back in that direction. So, I set my sights on identifying a college with an excellent journalism program. That, in turn, led me to a school right in my backyard—New York University (NYU).

With little thought to weighing the positives and negatives associated with going to NYU, I decided that it was the place for me. I applied, was accepted, and spent the next three years living in my parents' home and commuting to school. So much for getting away from home and going to a small school in a beautiful area.

I spent my time at NYU robotically going to classes and working my way toward a degree in journalism. By the time graduation day came, I could count the number of friends I had made on no hands. The graduation ceremony meant about as much to me as my high school graduation. There was one significant difference, though. On this day, when the caps went up in the air, I looked around and did not know a soul. It had finally happened: I had completely disconnected from life.

12 | CONFUSION

Not until we are lost do we begin to understand ourselves.
—Henry David Thoreau

After graduating, I found it extremely difficult to find a full-time job in broadcasting, but I did manage to get a position as a stringer at a local radio station. Mainly, I was a reporter waiting on the sidelines to cover a story whenever the station needed me. I did a lot of waiting.

Being a stringer turned out to be more of a side-gig than a job. It only paid on a per-story basis. As with anyone fresh out of college, the hope was that by getting my foot in the door, I would be on my way to building a successful career. It would just take time to accumulate the necessary experience.

Once I started as a stringer, the financial stress became unbearable because they don't pay for waiting, so I earned almost nothing. That created a lot of uncertainty about whether or not I had made an excellent decision to take this job. It was more than just the job situation that put me on edge. When I looked at my life, I did not like what I saw. All I could think about was that I was barely making a penny, I was living out of my parents' house, and at the current pace, my future looked grim. That may seem like a common dilemma for someone just starting out in life, but for someone like me who was battling depression and low self-esteem, everything was magnified and seemed worse than it was. I couldn't see things straight.

If I had been depression free, things would have looked very different. I had gotten a shot at a career in broadcast journalism; it would serve as the first stepping-stone for better things to come, and I was pursuing the career that I had chosen and studied for in college. The future was quite bright.

Unfortunately, my way of looking at things and making decisions was based on emotional, knee-jerk reactions rather than strategy. So, I did what any depressed person would likely do. Instead of finding some part-time work to supplement my income while I gained experience in journalism—I quit my job and short-circuited my career in journalism before it had begun. I ran away from everything I had worked so hard for without any logical reason or strategy.

So, what did I do next? Without fail, my trusty old patterns of fear and desperation took over, and I scrambled for anything that could get me out of my family and financial situation. I launched my life in a completely different direction. My new career choice looked good on the surface, but over time, it became a smoldering fire that would eventually burst into flames of clinical depression.

My next stop would be the financial industry. More specifically, the stock market—not because that was something that I was interested in or wanted to do, but because Mitch was working in the markets making lots of money, and he told me that it was something I would love to do and that I should get started.

Even though I still felt deeply conflicted when I was around Mitch, there was still a part of me that thought he knew what was best for me. I felt this way mostly because I didn't believe in my ability to make good decisions for myself—and so I ignored my feelings, took his advice, and did what he said, as I had always done in the past.

Forget the fact that I had not taken a single course in college having anything to do with finance, nor did I ever have any interest in it whatsoever. These were just minor details. So, off I went to the floor of the American Stock Exchange. In very short order, I was able to make enough money to move out of my parents' house. With this move, I hoped to bring some order into my life, but it didn't happen.

Going into the job, I had no doubt that working on the floor of the exchange was going to be fast paced and loud, but it turned out to be way more than that. The trading floor was total chaos with a lot of pushing and shoving as traders fought for the best spot on the floor to gain an edge over each other. And the noise level went way beyond loud, particularly when markets were volatile. It was total mayhem. I had underestimated how difficult the environment would be for me. There's a real surprise. After about six months working on the Exchange, I started searching aggressively for a job off of it.

Even though it is pretty normal to do some career hopping in your twenties, my decisions were driven by emotional uncertainty, self-doubt, and fear, rather than a thirst for new experiences and a desire for a higher quality of life.

So, I set my sights back on journalism. I had taken a shot in the financial markets and learned that it was just not for me. It was exciting to be back on track pursuing a career in the industry that had always interested me. The job on the exchange was just a minor detour. In many ways, it was a great experience. Wrong—I never even thought about going back to journalism. My takeaway from working on the floor of the American Stock Exchange was that it was just the environment that was not for me. All I had to do was find a position in the financial markets that fit me, and I would never look back. I was all set.

After about six months of searching for that just the right fit opportunity, I was still working on the trading floor and starting to lose hope. But just as my mental state was about to take a nosedive, I caught a break and landed a job in the bond market. Why the bond market, you ask? Because it wasn't the stock market, and it got me off the trading floor. What could make more sense than going from one job in an environment that I didn't like to another job in a similarly stressful environment in an industry that I didn't like? Brilliant.

The person who hired me, Michael, was a relative of mine—not a close relative, but a relative, nonetheless. To avoid any hint that favoritism played a role in his decision to hire me, Michael made sure to disclose our family connection, and he screened me just as he did other candidates.

All of a sudden, there I am in an office setting, sitting in an open environment with bond traders and brokers everywhere. I found myself surrounded by people who knew the bond market, had an interest in the market, and they were not as forgiving as the group I had previously worked with while in the stock market. It was a completely different mindset and culture than what I had just experienced, but still, another chaotic setting with plenty of noise to go around.

Michael was a brilliant person. He had gone through medical school and worked as a radiologist before running his bond market trading operation. Being a radiologist was never his passion. He had much more of an interest in the financial markets and enjoyed taking risks, which ultimately led him to leave the medical field. It was quite a lot to give up, but he followed what interested him the most and what got him excited to wake up in the morning. Not surprisingly, he quickly became successful in the financial markets.

In my position, I was a jack-of-all-trades working for Michael and with the other member of his team. As for my co-worker, Henry, he was never the most welcoming person. I think there was resentment from the start, stemming from the fact that I was a relative of Michael's. But way more than that, was that he had a massive ego and a giant chip on his shoulder. Henry had recently graduated from an Ivy League school and was the type of person who believed he was far superior to most everybody else because of it—let alone a person with an undergrad degree from New York University. It was quickly apparent that that was not going to cut it in his world.

Henry's primary responsibility was running the computer system that tracked our positions, the level of risk we were taking to hold them, and the profitability of our trading operation. It was an excellent skill set, no doubt. My take from early on was that Henry was indeed a very bright person, but his ego outmatched his intellect—significantly. Sitting between Henry and Michael made this conclusion quite obvious. Nonetheless, Henry was arrogant and condescending toward me, and this made the circumstance of trying to learn on the job even more difficult and high-pressured. If I had a question that I knew he could answer, he made it clear that he didn't want to help. He was annoyed by them, creating another headwind for me. It was uncomfortable.

Despite Henry's lack of cooperation and belittling treatment, I worked extremely hard and managed to become competent and effective in my role. Thankfully, Michael was always willing to answer my questions and provide guidance. He was a mentor, and I was extremely fortunate to have him. Over time, I was able to get over the rough start and gain Michael's confidence in my ability to execute my role effectively. And if that were not the case, I would have known it. Michael was a straightforward person. That was of the utmost importance to me.

At that point, by any rational person's assessment, things were going well. I was making great money. I was living on my own in a beautiful apartment in New York City, and there were lots of growth opportunities ahead. In short, the future was bright. And yet I was sad. Very sad. It didn't make any sense on the surface, but that's the way it was. I wanted out. The thought of hanging in there for a few years and likely making great money was not nearly enough to change my thinking. So here I was again, desperate to find something else, anything. But this time, I wasn't scrambling to find another job in the financial industry. Could I be on my way to getting my life back on a positive trajectory?

13 | BREAKAWAY

Don't let the noise of others' opinions
drown out your own inner voice.

—Steve Jobs

As I was trying to figure out what I should do next, I spoke with my parents about my desire to leave my position and exit the financial industry. They were vehemently opposed. And when I say vehemently, I mean vehemently.

My parents viewed the job with great reverence. They loved telling their friends about what I was doing and the financial success I was having. It made them proud. The fact that I was so unhappy in what I was doing did not fully register with them, which only deepened my sadness. I understood, in part, why they wanted me to stay. Financially, it made sense. But they failed to understand the depth of my sadness. In all fairness to them, I don't think it would have been easy to see it. I hid the depression well, even though I didn't know that's what it was at the time.

Although I tried to keep the outside world from seeing just how sad I had become, inside I felt all of the anguish that I was suppressing, and it was becoming overwhelming enough that I was opening up to the idea of seeing a psychiatrist. My mom had been encouraging me to see one for some time because it was difficult for her to understand why I wasn't happy, given the positive things that were going on in my life.

As for me, I was just tired of being sick and tired—tired of being anxious and exhausted all of the time, and tired from feeling sad and not really knowing why. I was distressed from feeling alone, helpless, and frightened, and worn out from not caring much about anything—I just wanted it all to stop. If a psychiatrist would help, you could count me in.

As I remember it, the referral was from a friend of my mom's who knew this psychiatrist. She was based out of Manhattan. For about the next year, I went to see Dr. Michelle Stone every week. I was looking for something—anything that could help me handle life better—and get rid of the anxiety that ruled so much of my day-to-day existence.

Dr. Stone did help. Mainly, I think just being able to talk to somebody that showed compassion toward me and wanted to help me feel better gave me a little sense of relief. And, perhaps more than anything, what I needed was relief, even just a hint of it. Those visits were essential to my survival during that time. They helped me to manage my relentless anxiety and the depression-related symptoms, but they did not resolve the disease. My mental health was not getting any better. Dr. Stone advised me to start taking Prozac.

Prozac had been introduced to the public about two years prior and was being prescribed by the millions. I knew nothing about the drug but had heard about it. When Dr. Stone told me I should start taking Prozac, what she meant by saying that didn't seem to register in my mind. I never thought of myself as suffering from depression. I didn't even fully understand what it meant. My visits to Dr. Stone stopped shortly after she advised me to take Prozac. I just viewed the drug prescription as a way of her giving up on me—that she didn't have the patience to help me get better—and she just wanted to give me a pill.

Of course, my reasoning was all wrong. But that had been the case for years. The disease of depression had skewed my thinking to such a degree that I could not see the benefit of taking medicine to treat it. Of course, if you don't even know you have a disease or are in denial that it is there, it might make sense that you would not want to treat it. As you can see, this invisible disease is crafty enough to warp your thinking and eventually drive you off a cliff.

In the meantime, as I was seeing Dr. Stone every week, I continued to struggle with the prospect of leaving my position at the bond firm. In the end, there was one significant event that led to my final decision. My relationship with Henry had become quite strained. As my confidence grew in my ability to handle my position, the need to ask him for help declined. I managed my role independently, and I think a substantial mutual disrespect for one another had developed. It's just the way it was.

One day, when Michael was out of the office, I had to make a decision about a trade that was fairly significant in terms of dollars at risk. Typically, I was not on the front lines when it came to trades of this magnitude. Michael was the decision maker. Henry was next in line, but Michael always had oversight and authority on the decision-making process. It was his operation. Nevertheless, he was gone, and a decision needed to be made. I could have easily moved forward on my own, but given the size of the trade, I decided to run it by Henry to get his opinion. I knew he would be a jerk about providing help, but what was most important to me at the time was getting it right, so I asked Henry for his view. Mistake. Big mistake. Seriously, a huge mistake.

When I asked Henry for his advice on the trade, his reaction was quite a sight to behold. He blew up and completely lost it—he just went off on me. Apparently, he had built up a level of anger toward me that was waiting to erupt, and the idea of having to provide guidance triggered the eruption.

Since Henry and I were in an open office setting, there was no privacy, not even the minimal level that would come with working in cubicles. The fireworks were on full display. He unleashed on me, yelling that the only reason I had my job was because of him. In other words, if not for him, I would have been fired long ago. His arrogance and condescending attitude were at a level even I had not yet experienced. His demeaning, cruel nature was laid bare. It was not a pretty sight.

Uncharacteristically of me, I fired back. My response was firm and swift. I already knew what Henry was all about, so his sudden meltdown didn't shake me. Well, maybe just a little. I said, "Hey, wait a minute, we are on the same team here. I'm just looking for your help on this one." My focus was on making sure the trade was executed and just moving on. It was quite the scene already. Ultimately, he took over the trade and tried his best to make me feel like nothing. He did it well.

Looking back, I wish I would have struck back harder. Henry had no excuse for the way he treated me. It was vicious and cruel. He knew it, and he acted exactly as he had intended. But at that time, I couldn't have acted any differently—I was already down on myself about so many things. I just couldn't understand why. The depression was over-taking me.

As unpleasant as Henry made things, I was very conflicted about leaving because working for Michael was terrific. He was always looking out for my best interests; it's hard to ask for much more than that. He made it easy for me to ask him questions and learn more. He just wanted to help me become better at what I was doing and share his knowledge. But in the end, I could not get myself to stay. No matter how much I tried to convince myself otherwise, it all came down to:

I can't—I can't do it. It's just not for me. I can't do it anymore.

There was no thought about looking at the benefits and costs of leaving, or what it meant to my future. I was being driven by something twisted in my mind. The reality was I was thriving on the outside but dying on the inside.

With no regard to what would probably be a significant bonus right around the corner, and against growing pressure from my parents, I went to Michael and let him know that I wanted to leave the position and try something new in my life. I could have waited to speak with him about the decision, but I couldn't do it. I just wanted him to know ahead of time. He had done so much for me already.

After I resigned and let my parents know I was going to try something completely new in life, their opposition was unrelenting. I often wondered what was more important to them—telling everybody their son had a big job on Wall Street, or my happiness. With the perspective of time, I have come to the conclusion that they truly wanted what was best for me, they just confused it with what was best for them. It happens. I am certainly not the only one who has ever been in that situation. Unfortunately, I was sick and getting sicker by the minute.

More than anything I needed support and encouragement. What I got instead was intense resistance. It was as if I was making the most catastrophic decision, and they were not going to allow it to happen.

Nothing that I said seemed to be getting through to my parents, so finally I wrote a letter to them to make things clearer about my situation. The exact details of the letter I do not recall, but the crux of it was simple and straightforward:

If I did not do something to change my life,
I would not make it.

Yes, suicide. I should have realized at that point that I desperately needed help, but I no longer saw anything clearly. Apparently, neither did my parents. I love my parents, but their ideas were no match for my depression. I had to leave and try something completely different. Surely that would put me on a path to happiness. Unfortunately, as I would ultimately learn years later, you cannot run away from depression. At that point in time though, escape seemed like my only option. My search for the path to happiness began.

14 | THE LAND OF ENCHANTMENT

You have to leave the city of your comfort and go into the wilderness of your intuition. What you'll discover will be wonderful. What you'll discover is yourself.

—Alan Alda

Michael was kind enough to give me the bonus despite my sudden decision to leave. The money I received allowed me to do something different with my life without the immediate pressure of having to look for another job. It was a chance to chart a new course—I wanted to try something completely different, and here was an opportunity to go for it.

I always had a desire to try my hand at writing. My interest was in short stories. Since my dyslexia and Duane Syndrome made it difficult for me to read books of any substantial length, I did the best I could in high school and college to read the classics assigned in American literature classes. I got through those books but gravitated more toward short stories. A couple of the ones I remember reading and enjoying were:

Edgar Allan Poe—"The Cask of Amontillado" and

O. Henry—"The Gift of the Magi"

These two could not have been more different from one another, but both held my interest start to finish. I admired how the authors could tell such spellbinding stories so concisely. And it was satisfying to be able to enjoy the assigned readings. No CliffsNotes needed!

Fully aware that it was a total shot in the dark, I figured what the hell; I've got nothing to lose. I might as well give writing a chance. While I began putting together some ideas for stories, I started thinking about leaving New York and living in a completely different place. Given that I already had familiarity with the East Coast, the Midwest, and the West Coast, I decided to explore possibilities in the Northwest and Southwest. After researching states in those areas, I settled in on two: Oregon and New Mexico.

First stop—Oregon. I spent two days in the state, visiting Portland and its surrounding areas. I just wanted to get a feel for whether or not it would be right for me. Oregon was beautiful, and the pace of life was much more relaxed than New York. I guess that would go without saying and was not all that surprising, but still, I needed to experience it firsthand. Another consideration was the rain. I was well aware that it frequently rained in Oregon. But again, I wanted to see what it would feel like to experience it. It was drizzling the two days I was there. The overcast sky and rain were not all that different from New York. A bit dreary for me. No doubt, Oregon was a beautiful place to live, but I left still wondering if it would be right for me.

Next stop—New Mexico. I arrived in Albuquerque, walked out

of the airport, and immediately noticed the big, beautiful sky; it was unlike anything I had ever seen before. It was as if God took a lid off the sky and everything opened up. Over the next two days, I traveled around Albuquerque and its surrounding areas. There was really no need to do it; I immediately knew it was where I wanted to live. Nevertheless, I was there and enjoyed driving around and getting to know the area.

One part of the landscape that struck me was the Sandia Mountains. They seemed to stretch across the landscape forever, at least that was my first impression of them. And what I liked most about the Sandia's was that they had a calming effect on me. Santa Fe was about an hour away. So, I went there to explore that town, too. It felt like I had stepped into a small world all its own. The surroundings were beautiful, and the town was filled with all kinds of places to eat, lots of unique shops to visit, and art galleries to check out. Back in Albuquerque, I used some of my time to see different apartments. There were plenty to choose from, all with lots to offer. Within a week after returning to New York, I packed a suitcase full of clothes, hopped back on a plane and made the return trip to Albuquerque. It was July 1990. I was twenty-six years old and on my way to a journey into the unknown.

Soon after arriving, I rented an empty apartment in a nice complex. Within a couple of days, I rented a minimal amount of furniture: a bed, couch, TV stand, and desk, and bought a couple of plates, a few eating utensils, and some high-end plastic cups. My big purchase was my first new car—a red Toyota Corolla. Red was not my top choice, but that was the only color the lot had left, and the car fit my needs. The state license plate read: The Land of Enchantment. And that was it. Very simple—just the way I wanted it.

So, there I was—all set up in Albuquerque. No friends. No family. Just me, a sparse apartment, and a few ideas to begin writing. When in New York, I was surrounded by friends and family, yet I felt totally alone and filled with sadness, and I lost all hope. Being entirely on my own in Albuquerque could not have been more different. It was peaceful—so peaceful. I felt liberated. Within the first few weeks, my mood slowly began to change. The fear, anxiety, and despair that had overwhelmed me for so many years began to lift. The person that I faintly remembered began to reemerge. There was a glimmer of hope.

I wasted no time in getting to work. Within the next couple of months, I had written several stories and sent them out to many different magazines to see if I could get any of them into print. I received numerous replies from magazines. Mostly: "Thanks, but no thanks." The responses were not surprising, and I never held any grand illusions that suddenly, my writing career was going to take off. I did get an encouraging reply on one of the stories; it was on the darker side of things. Imagine that. But the magazine didn't think it was quite good enough to want to publish it. They said they were interested in it, but it was a little on the weird side. That was it.

By the end of September, I came to the conclusion that, at best, the writing was a pipe dream, and staying in Albuquerque was far more critical to me. Better to get a paying job and continue to write on the side than wait around while the bonus money I had saved evaporated.

The silver lining was that I still had an opportunity to search for something in another field. And I did, but that didn't last for long. Not surprisingly, I chose the path of least resistance and applied for a job at a brokerage firm. I convinced myself that working as a stockbroker in Albuquerque would be a good route to go. Working in the financial industry would have to be much different outside of New York...I was wrong. It takes a particular person to make 100+ cold calls to try to get somebody to invest with you. I was not that person.

Despite feeling like I had made another fear-based career decision, having the job did give me some breathing room financially, and driving to work underneath the beautiful big sky and without traffic was a lot better than walking to the train station and then riding the subway to work.

I was feeling the positive effects of being free from the New York chaos that had exacerbated my depression. The need to hide my misery and pretend everything was great had quickly dissipated. My mood was improving, my energy level was slowly increasing, and day-to-day life was brightening.

And then it came—October 31, 1990—the return of Halloween.

I had not gone out to any social events during my first three months of living in Albuquerque. It was simply not my focus. I was ever-so-slowly starting to feel better than I had ever felt before moving to Albuquerque, and was content with what I was doing and where I was living. I did not want to disturb my peace and had no desire to start new relationships.

But on that night, the apartment complex was having a Halloween party in the general common area. For some reason, I decided what the heck, I may as well check it out. Maybe it was just wanting to reconnect with that happy memory of trick-or-treating with my friends or some other hunch, but I stepped out of my safe and quiet space and went to the party.

I took the short stroll from my apartment to the common area and walked into the party. I was not wearing a costume. To the best of my memory, everybody else was. I guess that would make sense since it was Halloween! But that night I could not have cared less. I was going there to spend an hour or two out of my apartment and relax. It was a regular, run-of-the-mill Halloween party. There were all sorts of fun decorations everywhere to get into the spirit of the holiday. I got a soda and a few snacks and sat down in a chair, quite content to take everything in and then be on my way.

But then this one young woman just came over and started talking to me. She asked who I knew at the party, to which I replied quite happily: nobody. I was not the least bit embarrassed about it, nor was I looking to get to know anybody. This night was for the sole purpose of being around people in a happy setting. Nothing more. After a few minutes, she invited me to come over to another area where her friend was hanging out. She could see I was on my own, and I thought it was kind of her to want to introduce me to people. So I figured, why not?

I followed her to a corner of the room by a window where her friend was sitting. There was a little girl beside her who was coloring the outside of a small pumpkin. Her friend was wearing one of those masks that is attached to the end of a stick—the ones that you can place over your face at any time. This one was a little different, though. At the end of the stick was a mask designed to look like a rat. It was placed across her face from side-to-side, covering everything above her mouth except for her eyes. Different, I thought.

Then, when her friend introduced me, she drew the mask off her face to say hello. As the mask came away, the first thing that struck me was the warmth of her smile. No doubt she was beautiful, but it was her smile that night that I will never forget.

Marie looked like she was about my age, and we started to have a pleasant conversation. Just small talk. The girl sitting next to her kept trying to get Marie's attention. I think she wanted to show Marie what she had drawn on the pumpkin. I was probably there for less than an hour, and we talked most of that time until Marie and her friend had to leave. As they were saying goodbye, her friend said they were going to go out the following week for dinner with some friends, and invited me to join them. Of course, I wanted to go. I wanted to continue to get to know Marie.

For the short time that Marie and I were chatting, I started to have a feeling that I was connecting back into the world. The flicker of hope still within me had turned to a faint light. Now, suddenly there was a sense of excitement about what may lie ahead. It was a great feeling— one that I had almost completely forgotten existed.

I left the party that evening knowing that I had just met a very special person. What I did not realize was that she was the woman I was going to spend the rest of my life with. But it did not take long for me to figure that one out. Within a month and a half after we first met, Marie and I got engaged. The following May of 1991, we married in the famous Loretto Chapel in Santa Fe, New Mexico, which is known for its miraculous circular staircase. For the first time that I could remember, I felt excited and hopeful about my life and my future.

15 | THE STORM AND THE SCREECH

*Fear not, for I am with you; be not dismayed, for
I am your God; I will strengthen you, I will help you,
I will uphold you with my righteous hand.*

—Isaiah 41:10

After some time, it had become clear to Marie and me that there was not much for either of us in terms of work in Albuquerque. Marie thought it would be fun to move to New York. There were many more job opportunities, and I knew a lot more people there, so that could be an advantage.

Moving back to New York seemed like a good idea to me. After all, now that I was married to Marie, it would be different because I was not the same person as when I had left. I would have her there with me, and no matter what happened, we would always be together, and that would be a powerful force for good for both of us.

So the decision was made. Marie and I would return together to forge a life in the very same place I had been so desperate to get away from just one year ago.

What was I thinking?

We put what few belongings we had into a small U-Haul that attached to the back of my car and set out on our drive to New York. We had a blast on the way there, stopping in different states along the way. The drive, however, did throw us a curve ball.

One night, about halfway through our trip, we were driving in Indiana. It was getting late, and we were on our way to the hotel we had booked to get some rest for the night. Then, it hit—a torrential storm. We were still on the highway, and the rain was coming down so hard it sounded like we were being hit from incoming fire all around us. I began to slow down, but the rain hit so fast I couldn't even see the shoulder of the road. I continued to drive at a slow crawl and then quickly glanced over at Marie to see how she was doing. Mistake. She was holding a string of rosary beads tightly, saying Hail Marys with her eyes closed! I was feeling a little uneasy before glancing at her, but after seeing what she was up to, my heart did start to pound a little harder.

So, while Marie sat next to me praying for our safety, I brought the car to a dead stop, not knowing exactly where I was on the road. We sat there together wondering when it would finally end and hoping—make that Marie praying and me trying to stay focused—that another car would not crash into ours. After about five minutes, although it felt like many more, the storm began to let up, and Marie opened her eyes and loosened the grip on her rosary beads. I had never been in a storm like that. It shook both of us up.

We made it through that night and spent the last few days of our trip listening to an audiobook of Stephen King's *The Langoliers* as we drove through different towns. We ate at all kinds of different restaurants and visited a bunch of tourist spots along the way. More than anything, throughout the road trip, we were enjoying our time together. Looking back, the memories of that trip are some of the best of my life, even the night we got caught in the monster storm.

When we got to within about a half an hour from New York, Marie and I started to get excited about the adventures that lay ahead. Our long journey was about to come to a close, and a new chapter was about to begin. We could feel it. And, as we approached exit 22, Mamaroneck Road, off the Hutchinson River Parkway—one I had taken hundreds of times before—my memory of growing up in Scarsdale began to surface.

Scarsdale is a beautiful town. It is also a very wealthy town. The expectations placed on the kids growing up there were extremely high. Going to college was a given. Of far more importance was getting into the best schools in the country—that is where the bar was set. Go Ivy or go home. It all made for an intensely competitive school environment, increasingly so as students progressed through the system.

While my parents were not a part of the super-wealthy majority in Scarsdale, my dad did well financially, and I had much to be thankful for. I was well aware of this at the time. That was one of the things that was always so hard for me to understand. How could I have been so fortunate, given so much, and yet growing up, I was unhappy?

I know that you are probably thinking:

"Poor Bobby, he grew up in a beautiful town with a great school system, money was never a worry, and he was expected to go to a top university. How tough he had it—give me a break. What a thankless, spoiled, entitled jerk."

I get it. And that is exactly what strikes at the heart of depression. The disease doesn't care about where you grew up, the size of your bank account, the reputation of the schools you attend, the level of success you achieve in your career, your social standing in society, your age, skin color, religion, and so forth and so on. You get the idea. In short, depression deals out its misery indiscriminately.

From the Mamaroneck Road exit to my parents' house in Scarsdale was about a ten-minute drive. I began to have an uneasy feeling as we got off the exit, and the reality of moving back to New York started to hit me. I remember telling myself over and over on that ten-minute drive that things would be different. Marie was with me, I would chart a new course in my career, and everything that I thought should have been great growing up now would be. But the anxiety came back. I hadn't felt it since my final days in New York before moving to Albuquerque, and just like that, there it was.

A part of me wanted to turn around and go back, but that time had passed. As we drove up to the driveway to my parents' house, I tried to convince myself that the anxiety would be temporary. It was merely a natural feeling that anybody would have given the significance of the change that was taking place. Wrong. Again, I would be wrong.

As Marie and I walked up to the pathway to my parents' front door, there was my mom waiting for us with a huge smile and open arms. Over her shoulder, behind the screen door, I saw the rest of the family. Everybody was there to greet us. My brother, sister, grandparents, aunts, uncles, cousins, and a few of my friends, including Mitch—of course.

As I entered the house, Mitch came right at me just as I had always remembered—his arms opened as his chest expanded, and his gait took on a purposeful, aggressive movement. Here we go again, I thought, as he got within a few feet of me. His embrace was always tight, not with warmth but with anger and intimidation. I am sure that somewhere within that mix was love, but of a warped type. I waited for his grip to loosen. As always, it was a relief when it finally did.

And just like that, the bully had his sidekick back. Life would now get back to normal. There I was again, standing amidst the chaos as if it had only been a day since I had moved to Albuquerque. I knew what had to be done. Back on went my mask.

Our arrival was late in the afternoon, and my mom had put together a dinner to celebrate our first night back in New York. Everybody was laughing and having fun that night as they should have been, but the anxiety that had awakened within me was once again growing.

Later that night as Marie and I settled into the room my mom had set up for us, I thought to myself, how the hell did I end up back here? At that point, it didn't matter. Albuquerque was gone, and I just held onto the hope that my anxiety was more of a natural feeling of this new beginning, rather than being back in the place I had so desperately wanted to leave just a year ago.

Within a couple of months, we found an apartment in Hartsdale, about ten minutes from my parents' home. Trying to find an affordable rental in a nice building was extremely difficult anywhere in this area, but Marie was never one to let anything like that stop her. While never intentional, it turned out that the apartment she found was in the same building where my grandmother—on my dad's side—lived.

Amidst all the craziness around me growing up, my visits to Nana's were always a respite for me. Her apartment was quiet and peaceful. The phone wasn't ringing every five minutes, which was typical at my parents' house, but on the occasion that it did, I knew there was only one person it could be—my dad.

Nana and my dad had only each other. My dad was an only child, and his father died of a sudden heart attack when my dad was in his early twenties. There were only a few other family members on my dad's side, and none of them lived nearby, nor was there ever much interaction with them.

If I ever felt any real sense of safety growing up, it was at Nana's. She was so easy to talk to. She understood me. Nana knew that being around the constant state of chaos that was considered normal by my mom's side of the family was extremely difficult for me. And she would validate that my feelings made sense.

While the rest of the family often dismissed Nana as somebody who just wanted to be alone, that could not have been further from the truth. She saw the insanity for what it was—abnormal—and had no interest in being a part of it. Had it not been for my visits with Nana growing up, I am certain I would have fallen into a depression so deep there would have been no getting out of it. Even worse, I would have ended up dead or in a psychiatric hospital for who knows how long. Thank God for Nana, both when I was growing up and for being there for my return.

It did not take long for Marie and me to settle into our new apartment, but both of us needed jobs, and fast. Marie ended up getting an interview with the Triborough Bridge and Tunnel Authority to work in their human resources department. She got the job, and in no time, was doing the New York commute—forty minutes give or take on the Metro North train into Grand Central. Then, a bus to Columbus Circle not far from Central Park, followed by a walk to her office building. Start to finish, typically an hour and fifteen minutes.

I was having more difficulty finding a job. I wanted to chart a new course in my career and figured this was the time to do it. Unfortunately, this turned out to be much harder than I had initially thought. Nonetheless, I had to get back to work, and so I had the not-so-brilliant idea to get in touch with the group I had formerly worked for on the floor of the American Stock Exchange. You know, that place I fell in love with at the start of my career. I had established a great relationship with the head of the firm before leaving and thought—why not, things are different now. So, I called up Randy and met with him. Within a couple of weeks, I had come full-circle and was back on the floor of the American Stock Exchange.

I knew from the moment I stepped back onto that trading floor that in my rush to get a job I had once again made a big mistake—but it was too late. Nothing had changed. Without any thought or hesitation, I fell right back into an-all-too-familiar pattern, including my relaxing, daily commute.

It was as if an auto-pilot switch was turned on in my brain—first, a walk to the Metro North train. Then, thirty minutes or so to Grand Central if I caught the Express. If I was lucky, I would get the local. That one was generally forty-five to fifty minutes on a typical day with lots of stops along the way. It was a blast. Next, it would be a relaxing stroll from Grand Central Station to the beautiful concrete stairway leading down to the squeaky-clean subway where I would wait peacefully on the spotless platform for the Lexington Avenue train to arrive. The best part was when I saw the train emerge out of the tunnel and approach the platform—slowing down as it got closer before coming to a gradual, quiet halt.

Okay, you got me. The final approach was more like an ear-splitting screech. It was as if somebody took two blow horns, adjusted the sound to a high pitch, pressed one tightly against my left ear, the other tightly against my right and then blasted them. It sent shock waves through my body. And yet, inasmuch as the noise bothered me, when I looked around at the other commuters standing on the platform, they didn't seem at all phased by it. They took the long screech in stride. No big deal.

While at the time, I did not understand why the sound of the subway felt like such a daily torture to me, years later I did. It marked the beginning of yet another symptom of depression—irritability, a type that went well beyond what would be considered normal. And, as the disease gained strength the irritability would rise in frequency and intensity, pulling me further and further away from my family and friends.

16 | ALL ABOARD

*That's the thing about depression: a human being can
survive almost anything, as long as she sees the end in sight.
But depression is so insidious, and it compounds daily,
that it's impossible to ever see the end.*

—Elizabeth Wurtzel

Throughout the next couple of years, Marie and I settled in, and she got to experience some of the happy times I had had growing up. One of the mainstays was Friday night dinners at my grandparents' house. The family would gather there at 6:30 every week, without fail. Papa would start the dinner off with a Sabbath prayer, and then one of the grandkids—we would take turns—recited the prayer over the bread. These gatherings were as relaxed as it was ever going to get on my mom's side of the family, and I gravitated toward them.

Then there were the holidays—Passover, Rosh Hashanah (the Jewish New Year), and, of course, Hanukkah. I loved Hanukkah. Eight nights, eight gifts. Couldn't compete with Christmas, but not bad for second place, and we still got to watch all the Christmas specials on TV.

My parents always had a Christmas tree, and there were always presents under it on Christmas day. I know, heresy, but who was I to complain? My mom would always make a point of telling us that we were not celebrating the spiritual component of the holiday, but I didn't even know what that meant anyway. I think she was saying it more to temper her guilt than to make a point with us. Her dad—Papa, was deeply religious and refused to visit our home as long as the Christmas tree was up.

In the meantime, I would join Marie every Sunday for Mass. While I never had a strong connection to my Jewish faith, I did believe in God and had a Bar Mitzvah, but something was always missing. Over time, as I went to Mass with Marie, I learned more and more about Christ and soon came to realize that he had always been a part of my life. I just never knew it. Now I did.

I was baptized at the age of thirty at St. Pius X Church, just five minutes from my parents' house. At that time, I did not speak with my parents about it, as I knew they would both be upset. I would eventually, but I was just not prepared to do it immediately.

The allure of New York wore off quickly for Marie, as did the excitement for her first job in Manhattan. So, as I once again searched for a career off the Exchange, Marie began looking for different job opportunities. More importantly, over this period, Nana became ill with cancer. Her decline was gradual at first but quickly picked up steam. My depression was already back in full force before we learned of her diagnosis, but as Nana became sicker and sicker, my depression intensified, as if it had a mind of its own and knew exactly when to strike.

My exhaustion level skyrocketed. A sense of loneliness started to take hold of me, and overwhelming sadness would strike without warning. And when it did, there was no way to stop the stream of tears. If I was around other people, I would find an excuse to leave as quickly as possible. No one could ever see me this way. Why? Because that might alert someone that something was seriously wrong with me and depression will never allow that to happen. In my head, I would hear, ever so faintly, things like:

"Bobby—you should be embarrassed. Look at you, how pathetic."

Yes, depression had a voice, and it was highly skilled at using it for maximum impact.

I visited Nana as much as I could as her health declined and as she became weaker and weaker. Toward the very end, she had trouble keeping up, and my dad got full-time care for her so that she could live in her apartment for as long as possible. I remember the last night I visited Nana. She had become very frail and could barely get up on her own, but her mind was still intact, and she always maintained her dignity. We talked for a while, just like we always had. I knew her time was near, but it never occurred to me as we spoke that night that I would never have a chance to talk to her again.

As I got up to say goodbye to her, Nana asked me to stay just a while longer. She had not once ever asked me to stay with her. Not ever. Just the opposite. When I would visit her growing up, Nana would always make a point of asking me if I needed to leave. She wanted to make sure she wasn't keeping me away from anything I needed to do. There was something significant to me about that. She cared about my well-being more than anything else. But on this night, for the first time, Nana asked me to stay. I didn't. I was given the grace to say goodbye, and I never saw it. It is one of the greatest regrets of my life.

Not too long after Nana's death, my dad collapsed on a tennis court from a sudden heart attack. There was no warning. He was doing just fine the night before, and nobody had any idea that there was a problem with his heart. But that day, as he was walking on the court, it simply stopped. Had an ambulance not been in the area at the time, he would have been dead, but we were lucky.

Within several minutes after his heart stopped beating, Dad was in the ambulance, and the emergency personnel were using their defibrillator. After several tries and about five minutes from the time of his collapse, it worked. My dad's heart started beating again. But he was far from out of the woods. He suffered a massive stroke at the hospital, and the doctors didn't think he was going to make it. And if he did, they didn't believe he would have much brain function.

After about five days in an unconscious state, Dad came out of it, and he was in far better shape than the doctors had anticipated. I remember sitting at the end of his hospital bed, speaking with his doctor. He looked up at my dad and then turned toward me. Then, the doctor just shook his head and told me it was a miracle, that he had never seen anything like it before. The road to recovery was not an easy one, but my dad rallied back and is still with us.

Soon after my dad's recovery, I was finally able to get a job off of the trading floor. Once again, I had a sense of hope. The job was with one of the largest investment banking firms on Wall Street, Salomon Brothers. Finally, I would be working in an office building, or as they called it on the floor—"upstairs." And even better, the building was within walking distance from the American Stock Exchange. There would be no interruption in my daily commute. And they say you can't have everything.

My role was to handle all of the stock options trading responsibilities for the company's high net-worth brokers. These were the ones that catered to clients with millions of dollars. The high net-worth department had carved out its own niche within Salomon Brothers and was successful by any stretch, but relative to the revenues of the firm, it was still not a huge money maker.

While the job was "upstairs," the environment was, in its own way, almost as chaotic as the trading floor. The office setting was a sea of open and connected work desks strewn across what seemed like a 100-yard office floor, from end-to-end. There were offices on the perimeter for the top executives, but everyone else was working in what I perceived to be a loud and extremely stressful, open-ended indoor trading floor. Still, it was far and removed from the dark, dingy environment of the Exchange, and for that, I was grateful.

Marie landed a job in the human resources department for the A&E TV network. It was an excellent opportunity for her. From a career standpoint, we were both on a great trajectory. Despite this good fortune, neither of us wanted to live in New York anymore.

It took Marie about six months before she realized that her dream of what New York was like did not match the reality. Not even close—which leads me to an event that I have never spoken about before. It is something that I was ashamed of at the time, and I still am to this day.

It is the end of the month on a cold, late February morning in 1995. This is the last chance for commuters on the Metro-North Train Line to buy their March pass without a penalty. Many commuters—like myself—wait until the final day of the month to stand in line at the train station to purchase their pass. The result is always a long line from the one ticket window inside the station stretching all the way back to the entrance doors and often spilling outside. Procrastination never pays. Any one of these month-end days can be a bit stressful, but you drop the temperature down to twenty degrees and combine that with strong gusty winds, and you are sure to get intense, heightened stress levels.

There are probably about ten minutes left until the next train arrives, and I am far enough back in the line that it's going to be pretty close as to whether or not I will make it. By the way, that was the other major stress contributor—some commuters would cut things too close and get extremely antsy if the line was not moving fast enough. You really can feel the heightened stress as the time to the next train ticks away. I will be late if I miss the train, but it will not be a disaster, so I'm not feeling stressed. On this morning, I figure that if I miss the train, so be it. Not the end of the world. But this time, things will be different.

I am waiting patiently in line on this morning not thinking about much of anything, when suddenly I hear a voice say: "Bob, I saved your space for you." I look up and about ten spots in front of me, there is my neighbor, Dexter, stepping outside of the line and waving at me. Dexter and his wife live a couple of doors down from us in our apartment building. Dexter is a naturally loud and pushy person. Every evening when he is walking down the hall after returning home from work, we hear two ear-piercing whistles just before he enters his apartment. Dexter's version of: "Honey, I'm home!" It drives Marie and I crazy! We never feel comfortable saying anything; we just hope he will eventually tire of it. He never does. He is a self-unaware person—no sense that his whistling is inconsiderate. Which brings me back to the train station.

From the top: "Bob, I saved a space for you!" shouts Dexter, stepping slightly outside of the line and waving at me. I look up and make eye contact with him. My first reaction is, "This is uncomfortable." I do not move, hoping I can just shrug him off. I should know better. Dexter sees me and his waves become more rapid and enthusiastic as he quickly repeats: "Bob, over here! I've been waiting for you! I saved you a place in line!" I am becoming very uncomfortable with the situation. We are standing inside a powder keg. One person can mean the difference between a commuter making the next train or having to wait on the platform, freezing, and likely being late for work. I do not want to be that person. I can sense the angst in the other commuters waiting in line. I can almost hear what they are thinking: "You gotta be kidding me. Now there's a guy with a lot of nerve."

It is hard to believe how completely oblivious Dexter is to his surroundings, but he is not going to stop until I walk past the people waiting in front of me and take the place in line next to him. Why can't he just leave me alone? God, I wish I never came back to New York. Almost four years since returning, and I am back in the throes of depression. I am as weak as I can ever remember. Alone and scared, I stand in line, twisted up inside trying to wait out Dexter. But it's not working. When will I ever learn? "Now what?" I think to myself. Finally, I can't take it anymore and yell: "Dexter, I'm fine where I am!" There, that is the end of that. Should be. But not so fast. That's what I am thinking, but I don't say it. The reality is that I revert back to the days when I would do whatever Mitch told me to. I am easy to push around, and Dexter, like all other pushy, bullying types, instinctively knew it. Reluctantly, I join Dexter. He is all smiles. I am tired, beaten down. I just want to get my monthly pass and remove myself from the situation.

Dexter gets his ticket and says he will meet me out by the platform. It takes about another minute to get mine, and I step away from the ticket counter and begin walking toward the door leading out to the platform. Before I take more than a few steps, out of nowhere a man comes, grabs me by the collar, and pulls me up off the floor so that I am standing on my toes. Without hesitation, he grips my collar tightly, looks me in the eye and yells, "If you ever cut in line like that again, I will beat the shit out of you!" He is not all that big of a person, but he is in a state of pure rage.

After the man makes that comment, he continues to hold me by the collar for a few seconds, and I think he's not going to be able to contain himself. I have no intention of fighting back. He can raise his fist, hold it there for however long, and then punch me as hard as he possibly can, and I will not do anything. I just stand on my tippy-toes waiting for him to either punch me or let go. He loosens his grip on my collar and then pulls away. I just stand there staring into space as he walks out the door and toward the platform. I felt helpless all the way through. No fight in me.

Stunned, afraid, embarrassed, and demoralized, I walk away from the door leading out to the train platform and sit on one of the benches that sticks out from the wall on the perimeter of the station. I watch as the train arrives, the commuters get on, and I hear, "All Aboard!" as the doors close. I slump over with my head hanging down toward my knees and my elbows anchored to my upper thighs. I stay in that position for about ten to fifteen minutes thinking about absolutely nothing, just letting the tears flow.

New York has taken its brutal toll on me once again. Some people thrive in the chaos and love it, but not me. Throw depression into the mix of daily chaos, and life becomes toxic. I was mentally and emotionally sickened from this situation and unable to pull myself together or show even a tiny hint of resilience. That was the moment when I should have realized that there was something wrong with my mental health. Instead, I blamed myself for the whole thing. I deserved it. He should have beaten the hell out of me. The depression was once again thriving. And, just as always, I couldn't recognize it. But one thing I did recognize: the situation was bleak. Something had to change, and quickly. Unfortunately, I was in no condition to make that happen.

Looking back, I now know what was happening. Prior to returning to New York, I was doing very well and had genuine hope for my future—especially with Marie in my life. Once I got back into my familiar family situation, all of my childhood insecurities were triggered and reactivated. From that point forward, instead of making positive and meaningful progress in my life, I was stacking pain and disappointment, the weight of which fueled the fires of depression.

17 | LET THERE BE LIFE

If you're struggling today, remember that life is worth
living and believe that the best is yet to come.
Remember that you are loved, you matter,
and never forget that there is always hope.

—Germany Kent

REMISSION

In the early summer of 1995, Marie's grandfather died. We went to La Junta, Colorado, for the funeral. I had gotten to know her grandfather, Luis Valerio, very well when we had lived in Albuquerque. He was also living there at the time. He was great to us. I loved Grandpa Valerio and wish we could have gotten to spend more time together. Still, I feel blessed that we were able to share the time that we did and that we could fly to Colorado for the weekend and be there at the funeral to say our goodbyes.

On the Sunday night flight back to the East Coast, as our plane approached LaGuardia Airport, I could see the New York City lights. Whenever we went to Colorado, coming back to New York was hard. On this night in June of 1995, it was especially so. Marie and I were now well beyond having had enough of what was not working in our life. Something would have to change. And on the next morning, it did.

Mondays have always been horrible days for me. The anxiety I had each Monday in my elementary and middle school years had never gone away and carried into my adult life. I never realized the connection between the two until years later, but no matter. I hated Mondays. They always brought with them overwhelming feelings of sadness and despair. I could never shake it. On the Monday after getting back from Grandpa Valerio's funeral, I was in bad shape. Hopelessness was beginning to take its full grip on me. All I could think about was when would this mental and emotional agony ever end. Of course, not until the depression is diagnosed and treated would it go away. Location and a multitude of other outside influences would always have an impact on the level and intensity of the depression, but it was never going to go away fully. You had to find its source first. Not easy to do when nobody even wants to talk about it, let alone acknowledge its existence.

Grandpa Valerio must have been looking out for Marie and me from above because when I walked into work on Monday morning, the entire team was brought into an office. We were told that our department was being shut down. Everybody was losing their job. While not privy to the exact reason that the decision was made to shut us down, my general understanding was that we were just too small a revenue generator for the firm. Beyond that, I had no idea. I assumed there was more to it. I did not care then, and I do not care now. Marie was not upset about my job loss either. For us, it was more of a relief than anything else. Our opportunity had arrived. It was time to leave New York. My second tour of duty had come to an end.

One month later, I finally made it back to the big sky of the Southwest. This time it was Colorado and the majestic Rocky Mountains. Marie and I settled into a one-bedroom apartment, a stone's throw from the foothills, and life began again. I had a renewed sense of hopefulness, and it gave me some much-needed energy. Of course, one thing remained the same—I continued to work in the financial industry. I needed a job, and the fastest way to get one was relying on my industry experience. So, I took a job with a brokerage firm working on a trading desk. I figured things would be better now that I was out of New York and in a more relaxed environment and with Marie. And, to some extent, that was true.

Soon after I landed my job, Marie got a job at the same company working in their human resources department. We started driving to work together, and for a while, everything was going along really well. After about a month, though, it became quite apparent that our morning routines were not compatible. We took separate cars, and we laughed about it. Within a year, I changed gears, taking a position to run a trading desk at a small, burgeoning mutual fund company.

It was a great opportunity at a small company nestled in an office building off the beaten path. While the job was very stressful, like any other job I had in the industry, I liked the people I was working with, and the partners of the firm treated me well. The office setting was quiet, and the pace of the day was manageable. All of these positives took just a little bit of the edge off of the intensity of the job itself.

Marie and I bought our first home several months after I started working at this job, and for the first time in my life, it seemed as though things were coming together. It felt like everything was on a happy trajectory. And for the next several years, they were. That is not to say that looking back, the depression had disappeared, but it was not nearly as prevalent. It was as if the intermittent bouts of sudden sadness, anxiety, fear, constant exhaustion, irritability, loss of interest in everything and everyone, feelings of disconnectedness, and general misery and despair had all gone into hibernation. Little did I know that the depression was waiting in the wings. It would soon awaken once again and unleash its force like never before.

The beginning of the twenty-first century turned out to be a monumental time for Marie and me. In late July of 2000, we found out that she was pregnant. We had been trying for three years, and several months prior had been told that it was never going to happen. Of course, a few months after that news, it did. Just a couple of months before, I had completed grad school. It had taken me four years at night to complete the program—double the time of the average student—and I was exhausted by the time I made it to graduation day. I felt good about the achievement, but it had taken a toll on me, and as my level of fatigue gathered steam, that feeling of irritability on steroids began to gather strength.

Jack was born on February 9, 2001. I was in the room with Marie for the birth, and it was like watching a miracle. We were blessed. And as I sat next to Marie in the hospital bed just after Jack was born, the sense of joy that any first-time parent would have at this moment was not there for me. That is not to say I didn't realize the magnitude of the moment and what a blessing it was to have Jack—I absolutely did. And somewhere inside of me, there was joy like never before, but I couldn't fully experience it. It was as if the emotion was blunted by something within me. Unbeknownst to me at the time, the depression was re-emerging.

18 | CANCER—WHAT
A RELIEF

There is no point in treating a depressed person as
though she were feeling sad, saying, 'There now,
hang on, you'll get over it.' Sadness is more or less
like a head cold—with patience, it passes.
Depression is like cancer.

—Barbara Kingsolver

In the early summer of 2004, my health started taking a turn for the worse. Out of nowhere, I began to feel an extreme burning sensation when I urinated. At first, I thought nothing of it. Just figured it was one of those things, and it would go away. But it didn't, and the pain worsened. Then shortly after that, just starting to urinate became problematic. There would be what felt like pressure building up, but the stream didn't start, and the pain ramped up another notch. Finally, when the flow began, the pain was so intense I didn't know what to do with it. There was no way to stop it. The only thing I could do was wait until my bladder emptied. It was a brief period of complete helplessness—just having to wait it out. I had been well trained to wait out pain, but this, of course, was quite different.

On top of these problems, the frequency of having to urinate was increasing and reached a point at which within thirty minutes after going, I would feel like I had to go again. Within about a month from the start of these problems, I finally realized that the situation was not going to get better on its own. I gave in and went to see Dr. Jill Pechacek. Dr. Pechacek had been our primary care physician since the time we moved to Colorado. A urinalysis was done to see if I had a urinary tract infection, but the result came back negative. Once this possibility was ruled out, things started to become a little more complicated.

A urinary tract infection was the obvious diagnosis, and Dr. Pechacek concluded that the best course of action was to refer me to a urologist. Within a week, I was in the patient room beginning my exam with the doctor. I described to him what was going on and that I tested negative for a urinary tract infection. He had some sort of scan or x-ray done in the office, and in the meantime, he proceeded to perform what I had hoped I was going to avoid. No luck. On went the glove and the exam began.

I knew it was going to be uncomfortable, but I realized that it had to be done. What I was not prepared for was the excruciating pain that erupted when, without warning, he pressed on my prostate. I screamed in pain, but the doctor maintained the pressure. I am sure he had a reason for doing this, but it must have been ten seconds or longer before he finally stopped. I just lay there, trying to catch my breath because the pain was so raw and intense that I felt like I had been through a period of torture.

In the meantime, the doctor was standing over me with a puzzled look on his face. He then just turned and started walking toward his computer. A man of few words, indeed. After reviewing the scan, he still looked mystified. The doctor was unable to get to the bottom of what was happening but gave me a prescription for an antibiotic and said my prostate was probably inflamed, and this would likely take care of it. After Marie and I left the appointment, she told me that my screaming had become so loud that she had her hand on the exam room door and was about to bust in and yell at the doctor to stop, but just as she was about to do it, my screaming ended.

Two weeks later, my symptoms were worsening. Now, in addition to the pain, I was waking up four, five, and six times a night. Whatever was going on was sapping me of what little energy I had. My overall health started to deteriorate at a rapidly increasing rate. Whatever it was, it was just taking me down. It was becoming unbearable, and I didn't know what to do.

Then, one afternoon sometime in November, I was working away at my desk as usual but had to step away to run to the restroom. Standing at the urinal after what had become the typical long delay, I started to relieve myself. Out of the blue, I felt something strange. It was almost like Jell-O. Reflexively I looked down at the urinal and saw a dark red blob. It shocked the hell out of me, and I instantly became very uneasy. Little did I know that it would be the clue that finally resulted in my diagnosis. Upon hearing this development, Marie took matters into her own hands and found a doctor she believed could get to the bottom of what was happening.

In early to mid-December of 2004, almost six months after my symptoms started, I walked into the office of Dr. Karen Taylor.

Instantaneously, we knew that she was going to be the one to get to the bottom of this. And she did. Dr. Taylor was a young, highly regarded urological oncologist who had that rare combination of brilliance and compassion. She recommended that I undergo a cystoscopy.

Having no idea what that was, I asked her to tell me more about it. Her description of it did not inspire me to want to move forward. I will spare you the details, but suffice to say, she needed to take a look inside my bladder to see if there was anything that was being missed thus far—that "anything" being cancer. The only way to get a look inside my bladder, with the level of detail needed to do this, was by getting a tiny camera inside. Something called a cystoscope would be utilized to do the job. To give you a little better sense of what I mean—think of something along the line of a colonoscopy but requiring a different point of entry. Enough said.

I had little interest in undergoing this procedure and, in no uncertain terms, let Dr. Taylor know it. She did not blink, saying it was absolutely necessary and the only way to rule out cancer, which could be the culprit causing my symptoms. Dr. Taylor reassured me that the procedure sounded worse to me than it actually was. She said it would be done in her clinic—meaning not even an outpatient hospital visit was necessary—and would take fifteen to twenty minutes from start to finish, and was tolerated very well by the vast majority of patients.

All I could think of was how agonizing the prostate exam had been, and this sounded worse. I was not inclined to move forward with this procedure, but as I would learn more and more over time, Dr. Taylor had this special gift of being persuasive even as it seemed as though she was just making a suggestion. I relented and agreed to undergo the procedure. As it turned out, I was not a part of the majority.

On the day of the procedure, I was given something to relax me, and once it took effect, Dr. Taylor let me know she was going to start. She did not get too far with that cystoscope before I began to feel a lot of discomfort. I tried to stay calm and get through it, but seconds later, as the cystoscope moved slightly further down its path, I erupted in pain. I probably blurted out some expletives as I tried my best to remain still and hang in there. Dr. Taylor stopped immediately and told me she would have to do the procedure in the hospital so that I could be sedated—which sounded much better to me. I think I was just in so much pain for such an extended period that by the time I went in for the cystoscopy, everything was irritated and inflamed—simply too late to be a part of the majority.

A week or two later, I arrived at the University of Colorado Outpatient Pavilion and the fun began. A nurse got me set up in one of the many curtain-enclosed spaces on the outpatient floor. On went the gown and the special hospital socks. A few warm blankets were placed over me. The IV went in—I hate those damn IVs. Then, one-by-one, members of the team that would be in the OR stopped by to visit me. They each introduced themselves, explained their role, and asked me a series of similar questions:

"Do you know what you are here for, Bobby?"

"Do you know why we are doing a cystoscopy?"

"Are you aware of the risks of this procedure?"

I remember thinking to myself, "I thought this was supposed to be a minor procedure." I realized though, that since an anesthesiologist was going to put me under mild sedation in an operating room, there was a protocol to be followed, so I just went with it.

Finally, Dr. Taylor came over to my bedside and asked me how I was doing. She was always a reassuring presence. I let her know I was ready to go. She smiled and said she would see me in the OR shortly. Sure enough, within a few minutes, a nurse was sending something to relax me through my IV, and then I was wheeled away to the OR.

At some point along the way, I asked whoever was wheeling me toward the OR to stop. Dr. Taylor was right there, right by my side at that time. I looked up at her and said, "Dr. Taylor, I don't want to do this. I don't want to do it." And I was intent on getting up and leaving. Not sure I would have made it too far, but that never crossed my mind at that moment. Between the time that the first urologist had me screaming in agony to the tremendous pain I felt in the clinic, I simply no longer wanted the process to move forward. Looking back, I realize that my depression was impairing my decision-making process once again. Dr. Taylor just looked at me, placed her hand on my shoulder, and said in no uncertain terms: "Bobby, you have to do it." There was something about the way she said it—in her tone—that I just knew this person was looking out for me. It was a clarifying moment. I realized I had no choice and relented.

The next thing I knew, Dr. Taylor was standing right there beside me again. Marie was with her. Dr. Taylor told me that she did find something but that it was small. She was sending it to the lab, "We just want to make sure. But don't worry, everything's going to be okay."

At that point, we went home and then returned for my follow-up visit the following Monday so that Dr. Taylor could talk about the results and the game plan moving forward. Marie was with me, and my parents had come in to give us support. The diagnosis was cancer.

No one wants to learn that they have cancer. The good news—the silver lining—was that Dr. Taylor told me that it was not the type of cancer that is life-threatening. It would have to be watched with regularly scheduled checkups because this type of cancer has a habit of coming back. If it did recur, likely it would again be low-grade, but there was a small chance that it could become more aggressive.

So, the protocol was to monitor for the next two years—each quarter going in for a cystoscopy. And then, if I got through those, it would switch to six-month intervals for the next two years. If I were in the clear after the second two years, then I would have to go through one more a year later. If there was no sign of cancer by the end of the fifth year, there would be enough of a comfort level that no further treatment was needed.

Even though the whole experience was devastating, it was treatable. The idea of a quarterly cystoscopy was not very exciting to me, but it was manageable. The prognosis was very good. It could have been a lot worse. It could have been aggressive cancer, which would have likely resulted in the removal of my bladder.

I was fortunate. My cancer was caught at an early stage and the small tumor was low grade. Anybody else hearing this news would have felt a great sense of relief. The prognosis was bright. But not me—well, not exactly. I did feel relief, in fact, it was a feeling of deep relief, like nothing I had felt as far back as I can remember. But mine was for a completely different reason. My relief came from having been diagnosed with cancer. I held on to the possibility that it would come back, and in a more aggressive form. While I understood that the odds of this happening were remote at best, the possibility did exist. I clung to it. If I could die with dignity from cancer rather than going through an untold number of years dealing with the unrelenting mental pain that consumed every waking moment of my life, you could count me in.

Looking back and thinking about my reaction to the day I was diagnosed with bladder cancer has given me a great deal of respect for the seriousness of depression. Instead of wanting to live with the disease in the hopes of someday maybe getting better, I saw cancer as an immediate way out. It was a twisted type of hope, an escape from the tortures of my mind.

19 | THEN CAME THE POLAR EXPRESS

*The gift which I am sending you is called
a dog, and is in fact the most precious
and valuable possession of mankind.*

—Theodorus Gaza

It was the fall of 2005. I had just completed cystoscopy number three. There was no sign of cancer, so the year was seemingly off to a good start, depending upon how you look at it. While my physical health appeared to be back on the right course, my battle with depression was not. At work, I was having trouble concentrating and focusing. It took volumes of energy to manage my responsibilities effectively, and at the same time, do everything I could to cover up my extreme sadness that came and went without warning. By the end of each day, I had nothing left.

But when I got home, all of my sadness was gone, and I would become instantly reinvigorated and excited about all the fun I was going to have with Marie and Jack. It sounds good—exactly what it should be like—but that instant happiness was not my reality. Inasmuch as I wanted to participate fully in their lives, the depression was overwhelming. I was incapable of feeling joy or any degree of enthusiasm, even for the people I love most. My self-esteem plummeted. I increasingly saw myself as a complete and total failure as a husband and father. My irritability soared. My anxiety level intensified. I craved time alone. There was a growing sense within me that I was not going to be able to hold it together. It was all happening under the cover of depression.

In the midst of all of this, there was still something to look forward to—Christmas. And this one was going to be special. Marie and I had been thinking all year about surprising Jack with a Christmas puppy. We both loved dogs and wanted him to experience the joy of growing up with one. So, with Jack about to turn five years old, we decided it was time to go for it. Though Marie and I never spoke about it directly, I think we were both in desperate need of hope. The puppy would be every bit about us as it was about Jack.

I went ahead and did some research on different types of breeds. We really wanted a dog who had a reputation for being affectionate, playful, and loving—one with a strong desire to be with family and a calm demeanor. This description, of course, could fit many different breeds, and Marie and I went back and forth for a couple of weeks as I picked out different ones that looked like they would be a good match for our family. We were having trouble making a decision, and Christmas was not far off. Then, one night, as I was looking through breeds on the web, I came across a photo and description of a Cavalier King

Charles Spaniel. I was immediately drawn to it, and when I showed Marie, she was, too. This would be the one!

I found a reputable breeder who had a litter born on October 31st that would be ready to go to their respective new homes right around Christmas time. The breeder had photos of the puppies on his website, and Marie and I looked at each of them. There was one puppy that immediately captured our attention. He was tri-colored—black with white and a little brown—and he had big, expressive eyes. We both knew he was the one before either of us said anything. I called the breeder, found out the puppy was not spoken for, and the rest, as they say, is history.

A few days before Christmas, we drove to the Denver International Airport to pick up our puppy. He was flown in from Texas. Marie opened the crate that the puppy had traveled in and reached down to lift him into her arms. As cute as the puppy was in the photo posted on the breeder's website, in-person he was that times a trillion. Truly, one of a kind. I didn't think Marie would ever let go of him, and as it turns out, she never did. Well, except for this first night. This one was Jack's.

Marie knelt down and put the puppy into our boy's wide-open arms. Jack had a joyful excitement in his eyes and a smile a million miles wide—one Marie called his chocolate chip cookie smile—as he snuggled his head right into the puppy's warm body. "Hi, Polar," Jack said in a sweet and loving voice. We had taken Jack to see the movie *The Polar Express* when it had been released last Christmas, and it captivated him. Jack knew what he wanted to name our newest family member before he even held him in his arms. The two would be forever inseparable.

Then, it was my turn. I cradled the puppy against my chest. His tiny paws rested over my shoulder, and I tilted my head downward, landing softly on his head. I could feel the warmth of his chest as it expanded and contracted with every breath. And best of all, I was just close enough to smell his puppy breath. That was a moment of pure peace and tranquility. I wanted to hold onto it forever, and in many ways, I did.

Christmas with Polar instantly brought a sense of excitement and hope back into our lives. He spent his days running around the house playing with Jack, following Marie everywhere she went, and even getting me more engaged at home. Quite an impressive feat! It became clear early on that Polar had a larger-than-life personality and a giant heart—both a perfect match for the big, expressive eyes that captured Marie and I before we even knew him. From the moment we all embraced Polar just outside the Denver International Airport, it was easy to see that he was about to become a shared source of happiness for our family. He had arrived just when we needed him. I do not believe it was by chance.

20 | IT IS NOT DEPRESSION

*We can ignore reality, but we cannot ignore
the consequences of ignoring reality.*

—Ayn Rand

Just after the holidays, I was back in the hospital being wheeled into the operating room for cystoscopy number four. By this point I had the routine down, but it did not change how much I hated going through the procedure. As usual, when I awoke afterward there was Dr. Taylor. She was always a reassuring presence. She gave me the news: all clear. It was a relief and a disappointment all at the same time. On the one hand, I wanted desperately to find a way out of the depression and be a part of Marie and Jack's life, but on the other, I knew what was waiting for me as soon as the effects of the anesthesia wore off. Without fail, the horrible feelings of anxiety were there to welcome me back—hard to find anything more loyal in this world than depression.

Three months later, it was time to do it all over again. And, like always, when I opened my eyes, there was Dr. Taylor standing by my side. But on this day, the news was different. There was a recurrence. In her usual way, Dr. Taylor was reassuring:

"There was just one, Bobby, and it was tiny. I am sending it to the lab for evaluation, but you are going to be fine."

Her voice always had a caring, everything-is-going-to-be-alright quality about it. On the surface, the news did not bother me. Instead, I had a twisted sense of hope. Perhaps the long shot was going to come in, and the bladder cancer would take me out yet. These thoughts were coming special delivery from depression. I know that now, but I didn't back then.

A few days later, the results came back—it was cancer. Not a surprise. My depression-driven thoughts told me how fortunate I was, that it would all be over soon. But there was still a part of me, weakened by the disease as it may have been, that had the natural reaction—it was a major setback. I had so much of life to live, so much time left to spend with Marie and Jack, and, of course, Polar. This healthy part of my brain, though, could not stop the depression from tightening its grip on me. I was now under full assault.

In the days following the results, my ability to meet the demands at work was deteriorating rapidly, picking up right where it left off just before Polar brought his jolt of happiness into our lives. I was struggling to be there for Marie and Jack at home. No matter how hard I tried, nothing was working. My desire to sleep once again became all-consuming. From the moment I got home after work, all I wanted to do was dive into bed.

On weekends, I would take three- and four-hour "naps." Then, I would wake up and want to go right back to sleep. One of the worst feelings I would have was just after I would awaken after a long period of rest in the afternoon, my heart would be pounding, and I could feel the anxiety bursting to get out of my chest—but it never did. I hated it. I just wanted to fall right back to sleep to get away from that feeling. But as long as I was awake, the depression was there.

I was increasingly losing interest in life. Once again, I started to crave being alone, and the march toward being completely disconnected was well underway. It was as if there were an invisible window of haze developing between me and the rest of the world. The depression was back and with a vengeance. And yet all the while, I still hadn't identified it.

As difficult as it was for me to deal with what was happening, it was devastating to Marie. She did not have a husband who was even close to fully engaged, and she was bearing virtually all of the heavy lifting that goes along with taking care of a baby. The situation was draining her. I was present, but absent. Something needed to change.

Marie urged me to go to see Dr. Pechacek and have her assess how I was feeling. I did. Dr. Pechacek had me fill out a questionnaire to assess if I had depression. It was not exactly a clear path to a diagnosis, but I met the criteria, and she recommended I go on an antidepressant.

It was hard for me to believe that I was prescribed psych-meds, but even at that point, I still did not think that I had depression. And every now and again, my doubt was reinforced by a faint voice in my head:

Just get over it.

Get it together and get going.

Everybody else deals with stress.

Stop being so self-absorbed.

What's wrong with you?

I devoted tremendous amounts of energy trying to convince myself it was just a matter of summoning the strength to get my act together, but this did not make the misery any less real.

While I told myself that I could use sheer willpower to overcome what was happening to me, at the same time I was trying desperately to hide what I denied was even there—the ravages of depression. Out of desperation, I started taking the antidepressants prescribed to me by Dr. Pechacek.

Two months later, I was not getting any better. The experience reinforced my belief that I did not have depression. But I couldn't shake it and continued on a rapidly increasing downward spiral. The depression had exploded, but I couldn't see it.

Dr. Pechacek urged me to see a psychiatrist. I thought it would be a waste of time, but I trusted her. Her office referred me to Dr. Camille Hazel. The weekly appointments began. So, too, did the stream of medications. One after the other after still another, I tried them all. Early on, it looked like one was going to work. I started taking an anti-psychotic drug called Risperdal. I learned that acute major depression could cause a person to hear and see things that are not real—hence the recommendation to try Risperdal.

Shortly after starting the prescription, my mind started clearing up. The anxiety seemed to ease somewhat, and oddly enough, colors looked brighter. For a short period, I thought, maybe it was depression, but then the side effects kicked in.

One evening, at a business dinner, I picked up my glass of water to take a drink. Suddenly, my hand started to shake uncontrollably. The glass was only about half full, but the shaking was so extreme that the water was getting close to spilling over the rim. I felt embarrassed and didn't want any of my colleagues to notice, so I quickly placed the glass back onto the table. But it was too late. One of my colleagues did notice and started calling me "Shaky Bobby." I tried to make light of the situation by just laughing it off—another one of my well-honed and self-defeating coping skills.

Over the next week, the shaking got worse, and I told Dr. Hazel about it. She was not convinced it was the medication. I didn't see what else it could be, but I listened to her and continued taking it. Then, another side effect kicked in—when I went to type something on my cell phone, as my finger neared the touch keys, it would veer off in one direction before it reached the letter I was trying to touch. That was annoying, but I thought, well, maybe it will just fade as my body adjusts to the medication.

Not more than a couple of weeks later, Marie and I were at a friend's house for dinner, and as we began eating, I brought my fork toward my mouth to take a bite of food, and as the fork got closer, it veered away from my mouth. Strange. I tried it again. Sure enough, the fork took a left turn as I tried to move it toward my mouth.

Think about taking two magnets, either both positive or both negative, and moving them toward each other. Instead of a force pulling them together as they get closer to one another, the force causes them to repel away from each other. That was what was happening as I tried to eat dinner. I did the best I could to get through the meal without anybody noticing what was happening and it worked, as nobody said anything to me.

At my next appointment, I told Dr. Hazel that I had to stop taking the Risperdal. She was still not convinced that it was the Risperdal that was causing the problem and thought it was helping me. Dr. Hazel tried to persuade me to continue with the medication, but I knew it was causing the symptoms. Pretty obvious to me. I stopped taking it.

After eight years of trying different medications, I was getting worse, not better. As the medications failed, I became ever more convinced that I did not have depression. Time and time again, I would ask Dr. Hazel how she could be so sure I had depression. She said that I met all the criteria, and she had seen hundreds of patients with the disease. She knew what depression was, and she was adamant that I had it. Of course, she was right. But I couldn't see it.

Twenty-three medications later, which excludes the variety of combinations tried, Dr. Hazel recommended electroconvulsive therapy (ECT). She said it was very effective for "treatment-resistant" depression. That was a new one. I thought to myself, so nothing that she prescribes helps, and now it is chalked up to "treatment resistant." How convenient. Very clever. I was in horrible shape.

I passed on the ECT, mostly because I had already seen it in the movie theater. I related ECT to what I had seen in the movie *One Flew Over the Cuckoo's Nest*. It was a terrifying scene in which the lead actor—Jack Nicholson—has ECT forced on him. It was violent and disturbing. It was also a million miles away from what ECT is today, and many people do respond very well to it. But I was not ready, nor was I knowledgeable enough to make a decision on it.

21 | THE GREAT CONNECTOR

It is amazing how much love and laughter they
bring into our lives and even how much closer
we become with each other because of them.

—John Grogan

Over the eight years that my psychiatrist went on her twen-ty-three-medication losing streak, the depression gathered momentum. And as the disease followed its natural progression, I was becoming increasingly disconnected to everything and just one step away from isolation and complete hopelessness—the dangerous end stage of the disease. In my mind I would be trapped in the complete and total darkness of depression. Blackout. I would no longer be able to see a path forward—the existence of hope would vanish. There would never be an escape.

There was only one thing that stood between me and the end stage of depression—Polar. He turned out to be the antidepressant that, looking back, I am certain saved my life. Polar was a gift from God, placed in my life for a single purpose—to keep me connected to life and to my family. And miraculously, he did—in ways that were simple yet powerful.

During the week, without fail, when I would come home exhausted after work, all I could think about was running straight up the stairs and into the bedroom and shutting the door behind me so I could just be alone in a quiet place. Of course, this would be the worst thing I could do. It would just separate me more and more from Marie and Jack, and make me feel like a major disappointment to them. As I sat on a chair in the room alone, the weight of depression would increase, draining whatever bit of energy I had left at the end of the day, and the desire to dive into bed and sleep would become overwhelming. It would be a complete downward spiral. And this is exactly what would have happened if not for Polar.

But Polar *was* there. So, every night, without fail, when I arrived home and walked from the garage into the laundry room, I knew what was about to happen. As the door shut behind me, I would turn and look out toward the far end of the kitchen, and there was Polar. It was about twenty feet from the laundry room door to where Polar was, and he would always be sitting in his trademark kickstand position. Polar liked to sit with his right leg extended almost straight out to the side. It looked like it was a kickstand to keep him balanced in an upright sitting position, the funniest damn thing.

Anyway, I would wait just inside the laundry room, and Polar would be staring straight at me. I could see the excitement welling up in his eyes as he waited for my signal. I could tell it took every bit of willpower he had to restrain himself until I knelt down and opened my arms. Within a split second, he was barreling toward me, and I braced myself for what was about to come because he did not slow down. Not ever. His head would smash right into my stomach and I would hug him and pet him as he kept bumping his head into me. Within about thirty seconds, our nightly tradition was over. I never tired of it. Polar gave me exactly what I needed—a brief period of happiness and peace. He lifted what little spirit I had left, and in doing so, kept me from falling prey to the temptation to withdraw from the night, never spending time with Jack and Marie.

And then there were those Saturday or Sunday afternoons when I would be in my bedroom with the curtains closed, ready to take one of my marathon naps. In the meantime, Marie and Jack would be with the neighbors outside enjoying the day. We lived in a subdivision with lots of families with kids. Our house was one of five in a cul-de-sac, a natural gathering place for everybody. I wanted to be with them, but the desire to check out from the miserable feelings of depression was powerful. I couldn't wait to dive into bed. But Polar had an even stronger desire—to go outside and play. Short of closing the bedroom door on him—which I could never do—sleep would not be an option. He was a very stubborn dog. Turns out, Cavalier King Charles Spaniels have a strong stubborn streak in them. Not sure how that one got by me, but I was very fortunate that it did.

So, off we went down the stairs. A brief stop to put the leash on Polar's collar, then out the laundry room door, through the garage, and into the sunshine. Just like that we were walking down the driveway, and there was Jack playing in the cul-de-sac with his neighborhood friends. Marie would usually be with their parents having a conversation as all

of them kept an eye on the kids. Polar was loved by all, and the moment
the neighbors saw him, it would always be the same:

"Polarrrrr!"

"Hey, Polar!"

"How's it going, Polar?!!!"

His tail would wag with such joy as he pulled me toward his adoring

fans, some waving, others with their arms open wide, smiles every-where, and Polar would dive into whoever's arms were closest. They wanted to see Polar more than me, but I didn't take it personally. They would have wanted to see Polar more than anybody. Luckily, I got to go along for the ride.

And just like that, there I was with Marie and our neighborhood friends, Polar by my side, talking with them—even laughing—and getting to watch my boy having a blast. Polar had managed to turn my entire day around—out from underneath the weight of depression and into the warm sunlight of a beautiful weekend afternoon. And he did it all the time.

Then there were those times once in a while when Polar needed a bath in-between grooming sessions. It should have been a one-person job, but Polar was big for a Cavalier—about thirty-five pounds. They are typically more like fifteen or twenty pounds, but somehow, his size fit his larger-than-life personality. Taking a bath was not Polar's favorite thing to do, and inasmuch as he seemed to try his best to tolerate it, he was always ready for it to end way before we were finished washing him. It was a job for Marie and I to handle together.

One of us would hold Polar steady in the tub while the other washed him. When the bath was over, I would lift him out of the tub. While he may have weighed thirty-five pounds going in, he was a lot heavier coming out. Marie would be waiting, towel in hand. But Polar was never interested in a towel dry. Before I could even put him down, he would wrestle himself from my arms. Then, of course, there were a series of body shakes as Marie tried to wrap him in his towel. It was not to be—water went flying everywhere, and Marie and I were not spared. It seemed to give Polar great joy and never failed to give us a laugh.

And just like that it was off to the races. Polar was anything but fast, but after getting out of the tub, he was an Olympic sprinter. Within the blink of an eye, he was out of the bathroom in full play mode. First stop: leaping onto our bed. Then a quick jump back down onto the carpet, usually followed by a brief pause to shake off some more water, self-drying. He was beyond excited.

From there, it was anybody's guess, but at some point, he always went charging down the hall toward Jack's room. If Jack was in his room, Polar would bolt into it and run by him. Usually Jack would be building Legos or playing Minecraft. Somehow Polar always managed to avoid the Legos, but I always knew if he made it into Jack's room. The sound of laughter was quick to follow. At that point, it was anybody's guess what was coming next, but the racing around the top floor of our house at breakneck speed usually lasted a minute or two. The final stop—our bed, of course. While our bed was getting soaked in water, Polar drifted off to sleep. He had given our family a few minutes of happiness. We were together. As it always should have been.

And then there were those nights when Marie would be reading in bed. I would usually be drifting off to sleep. It was quiet, but then, without warning, Polar would jump up onto the bed and get in his sitting position right in front of her. I would always turn and watch because I knew what was about to happen. Polar would lock his big, hopeful eyes onto Marie. She knew what he wanted but would try to ignore him. She wanted to read her book, and nothing was going to interrupt her. Polar would have to wait.

But Polar's stubborn streak never failed him—he would not move. It was a standoff, but it never lasted long. Marie could not resist him and put her book down. Polar had won again, and he shuffled toward her placing his head down for Marie to pet him. She did, all smiles and loving every minute of it. I would laugh as she pet him. We both knew it was going to end that way. It was a happy, peaceful moment we shared together—all three of us. Sometimes Jack would be there, too—the whole family.

I could fill the pages of this book with all the things Polar did that
helped me connect to Marie and Jack and to life in general. And even
though I did not fully realize it at the time, I did know that being in
his presence had a soothing effect on me.

Polar was a source of peace and calm in my life. While all the antidepressants I was prescribed failed, Polar succeeded. Only he was able to give me relief from the ravages of depression. No small feat. And beyond just connecting me to life, Polar's antics, bright personality, and abundant love drew Marie, Jack, and I together in ways not otherwise possible. He was the embodiment of hope in our lives. A Force. Truly, the Great Connector.

22 | SHUTTING DOWN

The greatest hazard of all, losing one's self,
can occur very quietly in the world, as if it were
nothing at all. No other loss can occur so quietly;
any other loss—an arm, a leg, five dollars,
a wife, etc.—is sure to be noticed.

—Søren Kierkegaard

While Polar was a major force against depression, he was not a cure. And, by the eighth year under the "care" of Dr. Hazel, I was on the brink of a complete meltdown.

It was October 2013, and the depression had reached a dangerous level. I was struggling to maintain my composure at work, but waves of sadness were increasingly overwhelming me. They would come at me out of nowhere. If I were fortunate enough to be in my office, I would close the door, sit in the back corner on the floor with my knees up against my chest, wrap my arms around my knees, and drop my head between them. The tears would stream down my face, and I would stay in that position, trying to keep my eyes shut and hoping the despair would fall away. Eventually, it always did, but not without consequence. With each successive event, I became more and more drained. Increasingly, the sudden waves became more and more terrifying. I did not know what was happening, nor how to stop it. I said nothing. To no one—not even Marie.

Not understanding what was going on since I had ruled out depression—based, of course, on my "Harvard medical degree"—I concluded that it must all have been due to the increasing stress and changes at work. The firm had been struggling ever since the financial crisis of '08 and, following a "reorganization" which involved layoffs and position changes, I was stripped of my title as chief investment officer.

Even as my mental health declined over the years, I had managed to move up the ranks. From starting out running the firm's trading desk, I transitioned into a portfolio manager position. Then a promotion took me up to senior portfolio manager, and as the firm grew, the founder passed on his role as chief investment officer to me so he could turn his complete attention to guiding all facets of the business as president. Even though I had made it through the layoffs, I was hyper-focused on the decision to take away my title as CIO and became consumed with fear that it was just a matter of time before they fired me.

Forget the fact that I had a positive relationship with the company's founder and was being reassured of my value to the firm by the partners; I got it into my head that I was on the verge of being let go, and nothing was going to convince me otherwise. That, of course, was not reality.

It was not a positive experience for me that my CIO title was removed, but it was not personal. The role itself was also eliminated as the company streamlined and moved forward. That was the reality, but depression has a way of making you hear a different story. In my head, there was a 10-alarm fire. And on instinct alone—my incredibly reliable instinct—I ran for the exit using my fear-driven, irrational thinking—courtesy of depression. You know, the depression that did not exist.

Feeling certain that I was within days of being fired, I could barely hold myself together and went on a furious search for the job that would cure all my ills. The energy that I was exerting just to maintain my composure at work was enormous. It was becoming increasingly difficult for me to keep up with my workload. At my year-end review, I was told that members of my team were commenting on my lack of efficiency. Hard work had always enabled me to make up for whatever challenges came my way, but now, not even extra hours could compensate.

Cracks were starting to appear. It was time to speak to Dan, one of the partners who always had my best interests at heart, about the struggles I was having with what I was being told was depression. But how, exactly, was I going to tell Dan that because of the debilitating effects of depression I had become overwhelmed at work and needed some help with my day-to-day responsibilities, when I was sure I didn't have depression in the first place? Quite the predicament...I said nothing.

While my search for another job was long, I was able to hold myself together until I landed a new one. And this one would change everything. At long last, the career move that would turn my entire life around. Yes, it was still in the financial industry, but a distinctly different path within it. I began working as an investment consultant for a rapidly growing and highly respected institutional consulting firm. My role was to provide investment advice to boards of directors responsible for oversight of public pension funds, foundations, endowments, and corporate retirement plans.

With this new job, I was 100% sure that the intense pressure of managing money would be gone. My anxiety, fear, exhaustion, irritability, waves of sadness and despair, and all the rest of the tangled mess of emotions would vanish—a thing of the past. I was wrong. But this time—catastrophically wrong. I was about to enter the abyss of depression. If only I could have seen it.

23 | THE VOICE OF DEPRESSION

Toxic People attach themselves like cinder blocks tied to your ankles, and then invite you for a swim in their poisoned waters.

—John Mark Green

The longer depression is left unchecked, the harder it is to treat. And sometimes, for reasons unknown, even when it is identified at an early stage it can be unresponsive to treatment.

My depression had now progressed to such an extreme state that the once-twisted thoughts that had wreaked havoc on my mind for so long were becoming audible. It was not like listening to the sound of another person speaking to me. It was more like the diseased portion of my brain was gaining power and starting to compete with the voice I have always heard in my mind when I was completely healthy. A battle was raging between the ever-growing diseased portion and the ever-shrinking healthy portion of my brain, and the latter voice was losing its clarity.

Exactly what was happening I do not know, but the voice within, which I now realize was the voice of depression, was real, and determined to take away whatever sliver of hope I was desperate to hold onto. For those of you who believe in heaven and hell, the voice is that of the devil. For those of you who do not, the voice is that of evil. One and the same, anyway.

While I do not pretend to be able to repeat word-for-word the dialogue that was going on inside my head at that time, I can remember enough to replay what it generally sounded like to me. It went something like this:

VOICE: You are worthless, Bobby. How many times am I going to have to remind you until you get it through your useless brain?

ME: I know it, but....

VOICE: But what? There is no "but." Look at yourself, you pathetic excuse for a human being.

ME: But I'm trying my best every day. I work hard to support my family. I always try to be a loving, supportive husband. And I always try to be there for my son and show him how much I love him. That is meaningful to me.

VOICE: Really, Bobby? Well, that all sounds so nice. So, how's all that going for you, Bobby? Not so good, is it? Working hard, are you Bobby? And you still can't keep up. So pathetic. It's only a matter of time before they fire you. Stop kidding yourself, Bobby. You're only making all this worse than it has to be.

ME: All what?

VOICE: God damn It! You are so stupid! Wake up already, Bobby! All the misery. All the despair. All the sorrow. I'm trying to help you. That's all I want to do, Bobby, is to help you. There's no need for you to suffer like this anymore. I am your only friend.

ME: Stop! Please, stop.

VOICE: Shut up and listen—all the pain, all the disappointment, all the sleep—what is it with you, Bobby? All you do is sleep. And you're terrible at that. You are nothing. Face it, Bobby, and let's move on.

ME: No, leave me alone. I can't take it anymore.

VOICE: You just do not get it, Bobby. There's nothing left for you. You are a waste of life. All you do is hurt everybody around you. You are just so damn selfish.

ME: I know, but I don't want to...

VOICE: STOP TALKING!!! There's only one way out for you, Bobby. Just one way.

ME: But...but...

VOICE: Shut your damn mouth you worthless excuse for a human being!!! Just listen to me. I'm going to end your miserable life...

PART TWO
UNRAVELED

I am now the most miserable man living.
If what I feel were equally distributed to
the whole human family, there would
not be one cheerful face on the earth.

Whether I shall ever be better I cannot tell;
I awfully forebode I shall not. To remain
as I am is impossible; I must die or
be better, it appears to me.

—Abraham Lincoln
January, 1841

24 | END STAGE IN REAL TIME

I used to think that the worst thing in life was to end up alone. It's not. The worst thing in life is to end up with people who make you feel alone.
—Robin Williams

DEPRESSION | END STAGE

From the first day I arrived at the investment consulting firm, I had a bad feeling about what I had just gotten myself into. I had run away from my prior job out of a false sense of fear without giving any thought to the specifics of my new role, nor did I think about the people I would be working with or the quality of the work environment. In the end, I had become beyond exhausted, and felt like a complete failure. I knew that I had to get out and had hope that this job was finally going to put me on the right career path. The work would be manageable, and I would come home at the end of the day energetic and excited to spend time with my family. Unfortunately, what I had hoped for and what transpired were two very different things.

Life at the new firm was everything but what I had envisioned. In very short order, that bad feeling I had on my first day had exploded. It was not long before it became unbearable. Each day was filled with fear, despair, and hopelessness. These feelings had been with me for most of my life, but over the last six months they had become increasingly intense. My new job was overwhelming, and trying to keep up with the work was taking its toll.

My ability to concentrate, which was always problematic, was declining rapidly. Tasks that should have taken an hour or less to complete were now taking triple that, and the work was piling up. Working late into the night, sometimes until 1:00 a.m. or 2:00 a.m., was becoming the norm and getting out of bed each morning, a rapidly increasing struggle.

My time at home provided no relief. Although feeling tired all the time was the status quo in my life, the level of exhaustion was now like nothing I had ever experienced. The only thing that kept me going, at least from what I could understand at that time, was the responsibility to provide for my family. Any sense of happiness that should naturally come from being with your loved ones was absent.

I had become completely disconnected from my wife and son. In my mind, even when I was with them, I was alone. They wanted a happy and engaged husband and father, naturally. I craved only quiet and sleep. I yearned for precisely what they wanted but had become a lifeless, miserable person. My inability to be a part of their lives made me feel like a failure. And this feeling was proliferating and sapping whatever little self-esteem and energy I had left. I used to say to myself, "I am running on fumes," and I did not know how much longer I could do it.

One morning, I ran out of fumes. I was trying to get up, get out of bed, and go to work. My wife had just left while feeling very happy, but for the first time, I didn't think I was going to make it out of bed. Up until then, whenever I felt I was not going to be able to make it out of bed, I would somehow pull myself together and get going. But that morning was different. I couldn't drag myself out of bed. I was facing the reality that my tank was completely empty. Not a single fume left.

I'm not quite sure how, but I managed to get out of bed and got myself showered and dressed. But even at that point, I was having difficulty convincing myself to head off to work. The thought of going back into that environment was overwhelming. It was an environment where I did not fit in at all, and I felt as though people saw that I did not belong there.

What made matters worse was that it was apparent to me that the partners who hired me were disappointed in my performance. I had come into their company with great promise. They had decided to hire somebody from outside of the consulting world. Expectations were high, and I was not meeting those expectations.

I had stepped into an environment where I was a complete misfit, and it was crushing me. I was overwhelmed with all the different things that were required for the job. Among them was trying to manage my scheduling for all the clients I was assigned to cover. It was a nightmare. The other consultants had control of their schedule—their calendars were organized, they made it look easy. Mine was a mess. I mixed up dates and missed appointments. It was extremely frustrating and embarrassing.

I was struggling like never before. Not even close. And I was feeling pressure like never before. With each passing day, it got worse and worse. As things spiraled downward, my depression intensified. I had some idea of the terrible condition I was in, but I was completely unaware that it was life threatening. I had reached the brink and not told a soul. And then, finally, the inevitable happened: I was catapulted into the throes of the deadly disease.

Yet even in this out-of-control state of depression, I kept trying to figure out how I was going to get myself out of the house, into the car, and then make the drive to work. But that morning, I could not imagine how I was going to do it.

At that point, I think the disease had taken me. My brain was gone—there was nothing left. It was the end stage of what I believe, if left unchecked, is a terminal disease, and so I sleepwalked into the bathroom, reached into the medicine cabinet and pulled out the Klonopin. I had typically taken a milligram each night. But I just took a handful and swallowed them all. I think I ended up taking somewhere in the neighborhood of ten to fifteen of around thirty that were left. I could have easily taken the whole bottle—I had virtually no sense of what was happening, but there must have been some tiny residue of rationality left in my brain because I didn't.

I went to work on autopilot. When I got there, as I was walking out of the garage, I saw one of the partners driving toward it. She saw me, waved, and smiled. Without any thought or feeling, I waved back and gave a courtesy smile. I could not have cared less about her acknowledging me. For some people, it would have mattered, but she was one of the last people I wanted to see. Smile or no smile, to me, she was a fake person. From the very beginning, she never reached out to me in any way, shape, or form that could be considered welcoming. Regardless of her reasons, I was sure that she and everybody else knew that the job was not working for me. I was a colossal failure.

I got to my office, which was across from the copying room. All day long, I heard the noise of the copying machine and people going back and forth. It was very distracting for me, not the kind of environment where I would have the best chance of being able to focus and concentrate. But there it was. Nothing was on purpose—I was given the office of the person who had left the firm. That's the way it goes.

I sat down at my desk and started to look at whatever was on my computer screen. Within moments I began to feel dizzy. I did not feel great; I did not feel horrible. I did not feel sick or nauseous, just a little dizzy. So, I got up to go to the restroom, and as soon as I stood up, my balance was off, and my vision was out of whack, making it difficult to see clearly and keep my balance. I was only about three steps away from my desk, so I put my hand against the wall, steadied myself for a second and then got right back onto my chair.

I thought it would be a good idea to take a few minutes to relax and shake off my dizziness, so I sat there for about five minutes before I got up again. This time it was worse. I tried to take a few steps out because I thought that if I could get to the restroom, I would be okay. I don't know what the difference would have been, but that was what I was thinking. I tried to take a few steps, but then my knees felt like they were going to buckle. I didn't want to risk falling, so I rested my whole body up against the wall, waited for a second, and then turned backwards and threw myself into the seat. I put my arms down on the front of the desk, rested my head on them, and just stayed that way hoping that whatever was going on would pass—but it didn't.

Things quickly got worse. My heart started to beat fast. My whole head felt not dizzy exactly, but as if I was losing my sensibilities. I knew I had to do something, but I only wanted to lay my head on my hands on the desk and try to let things settle down. Every minute or so I would try to lift my head again, but it just immediately made things worse. I stopped trying.

The dizziness became more intense. My heart started pounding harder and harder, reaching a level of intensity that I had never experienced before. It was not a panic attack—I know what that feels like. This was something that was out of the ordinary and much deeper and more severe than a panic attack. At some point, I became so disoriented that I didn't even recall having taken the Klonopin.

Still, I had enough of my sensibilities left to know that I needed help. Luckily, I heard the voice of one of the partner's assistants just outside my office door. She was the one person who had always been very kind and friendly to me. Reflexively, I lifted my head slightly, called out her name, and said, "I need help." She looked at me for a second, and I repeated that I needed help. I didn't feel well. She could see something was wrong and called 911, which was the right thing to do.

The emergency personnel arrived. I don't know exactly how many there were. They started asking me questions and put me down on the floor. Anybody who has had an emergency team come to help them knows exactly what this feels like. Those who have not, it is not all that difficult to imagine. So, they started putting an IV in me, monitors lit up, and they began trying to figure out what was going on. They put me on a stretcher and rushed me out of there and into the ambulance.

I don't remember too many details other than being loaded into the ambulance. But I do clearly remember one of the emergency personnel, who seemed to be the point person, kept talking to me and asking me questions, and I kept thinking to myself, "I don't know why he's asking all these questions. I don't feel like talking." But he was relentless. Looking back, I understand why. But in my head at that time, it was making me very frustrated and very annoyed. I couldn't relax, which, of course, is what he wanted.

I recall waking up in the emergency room and seeing my wife walking toward me as I woke up. She had a smile on her face. It was different than her normal warm and affectionate smile—it was sad. I think she had had enough. I had been through a lot, she had been through a lot, and this was pretty much more than anybody could take. But I think she was smiling because she wanted somehow to make me feel better. But I could tell even then that it was not a smile of happiness, and it was just a smile of sadness. I don't know how else to put it. She talked to me, I don't know exactly about what.

A psychiatrist came in—a very nice man. He asked me some questions, wanting to know how I was doing and what had happened. They were the kind of questions you would expect a psychiatrist to ask in those circumstances—although I was not fully aware of what was going on.

I noticed a security guard at the door, which did not make any sense to me at the time. My wife later told me the security guard was there to make sure I didn't go anywhere, or if I started getting up to do something, there was somebody there who could control the situation.

I was lying there, not thinking about much of anything. It was just—here I am, in an emergency room, where I think I knew I would end up someday because there were plenty of signs that my life was not working, not the least of which: I had gone years being told I had depression, yet I remained in steadfast denial. But the depression was never going to end simply because I did not want to accept its existence. It just went along its progressive, relentless path of destruction until it finally broke me. I was at a complete loss of energy, a complete loss of interest in anything. Really—just not wanting to live. I didn't know what to do. Nothing helped.

That's what is so sad about depression: you're sick, and you get sicker. It's hard to even understand why. Somewhere in your mind there is a voice telling you time and time again: "get up and go", "Snap out of it already!" "What's your problem?" "Move!" But try as you might, it's just not possible. You can't. No matter how hard you try, you just can't. That's the disease, it's just the way it is. Depression had now come close to taking my life. And even though I was still breathing, the disease remained very much alive inside of me.

So, that was the progression, and there I was. I really should have been dead. But I think I was still alive because I didn't make it to the final point when the disease can claim someone's life forever. Despite all of my years of suffering, there was still a small amount of light inside of me—just enough to keep me alive.

Lying in the emergency room, I felt calmer. Even though I didn't have a sense of what was going to happen next, I knew I was not going to be at work the following day, which gave me a sense of relief because I didn't want to go into that place ever again.

After the psychiatrist left, a different mental health worker started to ask me some basic questions:

"Do you know where you are?"

"Can you tell me your home address?"

25 | DLROW—MY WORLD TURNED UPSIDE DOWN

Sometimes the loudest cries for help are silent.
—Harlan Coben

A few days after being released from the hospital, Marie and I decided it was time to look for a top outpatient treatment center in our area. After dropping Jack off at school, we went to the first care center we had identified as a possibility. While it was highly regarded, after speaking with one of the representatives about their program, Marie and I, along with the representative, decided it was not the right program for me.

Onto the next one. Once again, we were impressed with the center, but their program was not the right fit. In both cases, the outpatient treatment program was not as intensive as we thought would be needed, given my situation.

It was a little frustrating because we did not expect that each center would not have a more intensive program. But the representative at the second facility recommended we visit the Highlands Behavioral Health Center. It was highly regarded for its extensive treatment programs. It was getting close to the time Marie would need to go pick up Jack at school, so she suggested we wait until tomorrow. But I wanted to go visit the center immediately, as I was anxious to find a good program.

I told Marie to just go ahead and pick up Jack; I would go to the center on my own. She resisted the idea vehemently, as she did not want me to go without her—she did not want me to be alone for any of these visits. She was worried about my state of mind, but I reassured her that I just wanted to learn about the program, and we could go together tomorrow if I thought it would be a possibility. Very reluctantly, Marie agreed and went off to pick up our now thirteen-year-old son.

I called the center on my way there to see if anybody would be available to speak with me. I described why I wanted to learn about their program, and the person on the line said she would arrange for one of their treatment counselors to speak with me.

When I arrived, I was invited to sit down in an office. Shortly after that, a counselor walked into the office and shut the door. I immediately began describing to her the events that had eventually led me to the center and told her I wanted to learn about their outpatient treatment program.

As I look back on that meeting, one thing that had not even crossed my mind as we began our discussion was that instead of telling me about their program, the counselor started to ask a lot of questions, all aimed at digging deeper into understanding my current state of mind. I answered her questions honestly, as I thought it was vital for her to know just how down I was about life. In my mind, it made sense that she would want to know more so she could provide informed professional advice about whether or not their program would be appropriate for me.

After about twenty minutes of questioning, she excused herself from the room and said she would be back shortly. As the door closed behind her, I sat alone thinking about everything that had transpired and the despair that had led me to exactly where I was. A wave of sadness came over me, one I had felt all too many times. My eyes welled up with tears. Thoughts of all the pain I had caused my wife and son came crashing down on me. The fear and anxiety of being swept up by sorrow and not knowing when it was going to end enveloped me. I wanted it to stop but had no control over when it would. Over and over and over again, this wave would come rushing at me, and the despair it always brought with it had become intolerable.

I put my elbows on the table, closed my eyes, put my hands over my face, and waited. At some point, it would subside, but I never knew when. It was frightening and exhausting. Time stopped as I was in the midst of this event. It always did. Slowly, the wave receded. It had taxed my mental and physical state dramatically. As the event began to fade, I heard the door open, and the counselor walked in with another person. I did not know who he was or why he was there, but he sat down near me and began asking me questions:

"Do you have a lot of anxiety?"

"Do you have feelings of despair?"

"Do you have feelings of shame? Of guilt?"

"Do you feel overwhelmed?"

"Do you feel helpless?"

"Do you feel hopeless?"

My answers were no surprise—seven yeses. All of these feelings consumed my existence. My mood fell lower and lower with every response. Then, the man asked the most important question of all: Do you ever have thoughts of suicide? The short answer was yes, but I hesitated because it just felt like this whole meeting was now going in a direction that had nothing to do with their outpatient treatment program.

This time, I hedged on my answer by simply saying: "I don't know." Then, he asked me one last question. Where it came from or why it was necessary was a mystery to me at the time, but he asked it:

"Bobby, can you spell the word 'world' backward for me?"

I should have spelled it "dlrow," but whether or not I reverse-spelled it correctly, I do not know. Perhaps I didn't, and that partly contributed to the events that quickly transpired. I will never know for certain, but after a brief pause, he asked me for the name of my psychiatrist. I gave him her name. He asked me if it would be okay if he called her. I said, "Sure." He walked out of the room, and I never saw him again. What happened next would shatter my entire life and alter its trajectory forever.

26 | THE TURNING POINT

I may not have gone where I intended to go,
but I think I have ended up where I needed to be.
—Douglas Adams

The next thing I remember, I was standing with my back to a nurse's station. In front of me was an open area. I looked around, trying to get my bearings. Patients were walking all around in front of me. Off to my right was a couch where people were playing a board game. Looking out to my left, there was a hallway with doors leading to rooms on either side. At the end of the hall was a large window with a couple of chairs in front of it. No curtains. I just stood there, frozen, gazing at my surroundings. Nothing made sense. I felt alone, afraid, sad, ashamed, and maybe most of all, powerless. I was stuck, and there wasn't a damn thing I could do about it. I had reached my all-time low, and that is a long, long way down.

Then, I heard a voice coming from behind me. One of the nurses was trying to get my attention. When I turned around, I saw that she was holding a bag with clothes in it. Marie had dropped them off for me. The nurse looked through the clothes carefully and pulled out a pair of sweatpants. Then, she proceeded to slowly remove the drawstring before putting the sweatpants back in the bag and handing it to me. That was the moment everything became real. I was shell-shocked: I had reached my all-time low. Again. That did not take long.

One of the staff members escorted me to my room and said he would be back shortly. The room was simple—two basic twin beds and two open-shelved, wooden dressers with a small table and chair in-between them—no sharp edges on the furniture. All of the furniture was made of a light wood—something calming about it. There was a large window. No curtain. It looked like the bottom half was tinted. I went over to it and looked out—I seemed to be on the second floor of the building. I knocked on the glass. It was thick. I knocked harder just to see what would happen. I had no idea what kind of glass it was, but it became immediately apparent—a hand would break before the glass ever did.

The walls were blank—except for a picture, I think of a landscape. There was a small bathroom—no mirror—with a shower and a sink. To get water, you had to push down on a round metal piece on top of the back end of the faucet. It rose slightly above, almost like a small half bubble. I pushed down on it. Water started streaming from the faucet. It did not last long. And that was it.

The place had a minimalist feel to it. If it had not been for the absence of a television, I could have almost been back in my apartment in Albuquerque. If nothing else, the room was quiet, and I was glad to be away from the open area. After putting my clothes in the open shelves, I sat down on the bed and waited. In no time at all, the staff member returned and led me back out to the open area. It was time for dinner.

The patients had gathered in the open space and went in groups to the elevators. The cafeteria was one floor down—ground level. When I walked in, it seemed like an ordinary school cafeteria. Of course, there was a slight difference. No surprise, the utensils were plastic and only forks and spoons. The meals were served on Styrofoam plates, and the cups—also Styrofoam. I got my food and sat down at a table at the far end of the room against the wall. There were just two seats, and I wanted to be away from everybody else. When I went to pull the chair out from the table, I was surprised. It was heavy. There was a brief time delay in my brain before I realized what that was all about.

After a short time, one of the staff members asked if anybody wanted to go outside. A small group was led through a door leading out to a courtyard. I could see it. Some of the patients went out to smoke a cigarette, others just to get some fresh air. The courtyard was enclosed, but there was plenty of space.

After dinner, everybody lined up to head back to the elevators and up to our floor. The staff watched as everybody threw everything in the garbage. Nothing left the cafeteria. As I recall, there was a break where everybody went back to their rooms for a short period. Then, it was free time. The unit had a social room where everybody gathered. There was a TV mounted against the wall. There were couches, chairs, and tables. Some patients were talking, others playing cards or board games, still others worked on puzzles together. I have no idea what I was doing. Probably just walking around aimlessly. As the evening went on, a staff member announced it was snack time. Everybody lined up in front of a refrigerator. One-by-one, each person was given a carton of Jell-O or pudding. There may have been other snacks, but that is all I remember. I just watched.

The final item on the agenda before bed was taking meds. Once again, everybody stood in a line, this time in front of a closed cabinet. The door of the cabinet swung open, a staff member was on the other side. One-by-one, each person got their evening dose. The staffer would place them in a tiny pill cup and watch to make sure they were swallowed.

When it was finally my turn, I got my meds. Klonopin helped me sleep. Yes, of all things, they gave me Klonopin. Being in a controlled environment made it safe, I guess. They also had my Lamictal; it was supposed to help me with depression and dampening mood swings. Then, it was back to my room and lights out. My first day in the inpatient unit had come to a close. It still had not hit me. There was no way I belonged there. I just had to get through it and be on my way.

Even with the Klonopin, I was having trouble getting to sleep. Eventually, I dozed off, but sometime after I finally fell asleep, I was awoken by what sounded like footsteps. I turned my head, and sure enough, a staff member was coming toward me. It was dark, so I couldn't see who it was but figured it had to be a staff member. I was half asleep, anyway. Then, next thing I know, there was a red laser light shining on my face. What the hell was going on? But then, within a matter of seconds, he was gone. I had a very uneasy feeling. Whatever had just happened startled me, but I was so groggy from the Klonopin that I quickly fell back to sleep. I desperately wanted to sleep—it was my only way out.

But they did not make it easy to sleep. Every time I started to drift off I would hear footsteps, followed shortly thereafter by the red laser light in my face. It seemed like it would occur every fifteen or twenty minutes. I didn't understand what was going on, but I just wanted it to stop. It was scaring me.

I finally managed to get some sleep. The Klonopin must have eventually kicked in. When I woke up that first morning, I was afraid. Pretty pathetic, a fifty-one-year-old man held in a mental health facility, placed in a room designed to protect me from myself, and now standing in front of the window, staring out and trembling like a little boy. If there were ever any doubt about how depression can destroy a person, the condition I was in that first morning in my room should have put it to rest. And yet, at that moment, astonishingly, I was still of the mindset that my current condition of feeling completely stressed, scared, and overwhelmed was directly related to the whole shocking experience of how I ended up in the Highlands Behavioral Center, rather than the reality that those were the symptoms of my depression. I was in severe and steadfast depression denial.

At some point, a staff member walked into my room and said it was time to go downstairs for breakfast. I sleepwalked to the cafeteria, got a cup of coffee, and took a seat at the same table where I had had dinner the night before. I just wanted to be alone and get through this, however long it was going to take to do my time and get the hell out of there. But that mindset was just about to change. It was time for the first class on the daily schedule:

Group therapy: The emotional check-in.

27 | THE CURTAIN FALLS

Adversity is like a strong wind. It tears away
from us all but the things that cannot be torn,
so that we see ourselves as we really are.

—Arthur Golden

I walked into my first class in the inpatient unit. It was a group therapy session, and there were about fifteen of us sitting around a rectangular table. The therapist handed each of us a sheet with lots of questions related to how we were feeling. Then, she started going around the table, asking the first question:

"How would you rate your depression this morning on a scale of one to ten?"

Ten meant that your depression was through the roof. One signaled that you were feeling depression-free.

The numbers were high—mainly eights and nines, even a ten here and there. Apparently, I had made the all-star team. While I do not recall what number I saw myself as that morning, it is safe to assume that it was north of ten.

I watched and listened as, one-by-one, each person spoke, revealing their level of depression and elaborating on what seemed to be driving their state of mind. Their voices were filled with deep sadness. Where did the sadness come from? I got the impression that nobody knew— it was just there. Something unidentifiable was weighing down on everybody. Nobody could shake it. I could feel the exhaustion in their voices and see it in their stilted body movements. Everything I had felt for so long was right there in front of me. It was like I saw a reflection of myself on each one of their faces.

My turn was coming, but I was not even thinking about it. I knew nothing about these people other than that they were clearly of different ages, backgrounds, and ethnicities. As each of them responded to the question—as strange as this may sound—I almost instantly felt like somehow, I had known each one of them. They all had a look of total despair written all over their faces. And as each patient described their level of depression, the despair became increasingly visible.

Yes—I can hear you, I thought to myself; I see, feel, and relate to your despair. Then I asked myself a simple question:

Bobby, how do you know what despair looks like?

All I can say is that despair has been a part of my life since childhood, and its intensity increased at a faster and faster pace with each passing year before it finally overcame me and dropped me right down into the abyss of hopelessness.

I know what sad looks like. Everybody experiences sadness at one time or another—we all know the face of sadness when we see it. A small percentage of people experience the magnitude and depth of despair that is one of the hallmarks of depression. We know the face of despair when we see it.

But I saw and heard far more than just despair in that room. There was misery, anguish, guilt, shame, worthlessness, helplessness, and the ever-present overhang of hopelessness everywhere. It all filled the room. Essentially, overwhelming human suffering. Needless to say, there were lots of tears to go around. Mine included. I thought this place was supposed to make me feel better.

And then it was my turn. I told them my level of depression and said little else. I was uneasy and extremely distracted. I simply could not get over how everything in that room was making me feel.

Inasmuch as over the years I had come to distrust Dr. Hazel and her assertion that I had depression, I could not deny what was all around me. Everything I saw on their faces, heard in their voices, and recognized in their descriptions of depression exactly mirrored my own life experience. And just like that, the curtain fell. There was no escaping it. All this time, it had been depression. The reality quickly sunk in, but instead of falling into a darker place, I felt a sense of relief. In the first class of the first day of my inpatient stay, my depression was unmasked. At long last, I could see my enemy.

28 | FINALLY, AFTER 45 YEARS

The loneliest moment in someone's life is when
they are watching their whole world fall apart,
and all they can do is stare blankly.
—F. Scott Fitzgerald

The rest of the day was filled with different classes designed to provide a variety of coping skills. I went through the motions, still feeling the aftershocks of how I had ended up in the Highlands.

Dinner was just like the first night. I still did not know anybody and was resisting letting myself give into the situation. There was no reason for me to have been forced into this place. Engaging in anything would be me admitting that I belonged here. It was not going to happen.

That night, the red laser light returned—shining in my face each time I started to doze off. It was unsettling, but I had learned earlier in the day that it was a standard routine. My understanding was that a team of staff members were assigned to monitor all patients at fifteen-minute intervals throughout the night. The reason for the consistent checks was to ensure the safety of each patient. Inasmuch as the hospital tried to take every possible precaution to do this, patients could get very creative in finding ways to harm themselves.

For the same reason, no patient was ever left alone for more than a few minutes during the day. There were a number of times when I went back to my room if there was a break during the schedule of classes, and within five minutes, without fail, a staff member would walk in to see what I was doing. It became quickly apparent why when I first entered the inpatient unit, somebody at the nurse's desk immediately took a photo of me. Every staff member had copies of my photo, as well as every other patient, so they could keep tabs on us throughout the day.

My second day in the unit began with a repeat of the emotional check-in. The reality of my depression was confirmed. It hacked away at my belief that I did not belong in this hospital. I would have none of it. More classes throughout the day focused on providing everybody with skills to help cope with depression in our day-to-day life.

At dinner that evening, it was back to my table away from everybody. My body language shouted, "Leave me alone." They did.

Next—the nightly social hour before lights went out. Included with this part of the evening was the opportunity for each patient to make a call. There was a board that showed the rotation. As I recall, each person got about five to ten minutes.

The first two nights, I spoke with Marie. She was worried that they were going to hold me there for who knows how long. It was as if she thought I was being held in prison. Not comforting, but as hard as it was for me in some ways, I think it was even tougher on her. She was trying to reassure me that she was working on getting me out of there, while at the same time trying to maintain her composure for Jack. It must have been extremely difficult.

On the third night, Marie put Jack on the phone. He wanted to talk to me.

"Jack?"

"Hi, Daddy," he said with a voice that was strained.

"Hi, Jack. How are you doing?"

"When are you coming home, Daddy?" I could hear his distress.

"I'll be home very soon. Probably a couple of days." I had no idea.

"Everything is going to be okay, Jack. They just want me here temporarily. Try not to worry. I promise everything is going to be okay." I was trying my best to reassure him, but Jack is a smart boy. He knew something was very wrong.

"Please come home, Daddy...." Before I could say anything, I heard Jack say, "Here, Mommy," as his voice faded away.

There was no more time left to talk. I didn't want to, anyway. I said good night to Marie and hung up.

I walked into the social room and sat down on the floor again. For the next what must have been fifteen to twenty minutes, I stared into nowhere, as my short conversation with Jack consumed my thoughts. The damage I had caused him was immeasurable. All I wanted to do was take Jack in my arms and tell him how much I loved him and that he had nothing to worry about. But it is tough to pretend that everything is going to be just fine when I knew we were already well beyond that point.

How was I ever going to put my life back together and make up for what I had done? No answers. Nothing made sense anymore. I have never felt lonelier than I did at that moment. There was no distant second. It was in a category all its own. Depression saw the opening and ran with it, with great joy:

"You are a loser, Bobby, a weak, pathetic excuse for a human being. Just think about what you have just done to your son. He will never be the same. You ought to be ashamed of yourself."

I likely would have remained as I was for an untold amount of time, or at least until the staff shut things down for the night. There was no end in sight. But then, out of the corner of my left eye, I saw a glimpse of somebody coming toward me. At first, I paid little attention to it, but she was moving in my direction and had what seemed like a spring in her step. No way she could be approaching me, but I put on my leave-me-alone body language, just in case. She came to a stop right next to me and sat down. Without hesitation, Kaylie introduced herself and attempted to engage me in a conversation. Short of being extremely rude, I was stuck—quite the predicament.

I dropped my guard and responded, introducing myself to her. Kaylie looked like she was in her early twenties and could not have been nicer. She told me about why she was in the Highlands, and I spoke with her about how I ended up there. For the first time since entering the Highlands, I began to feel at ease. First, there was the realization that I had depression. Now, for the first time in my life, I had spoken with another person who suffered from it. It took forty-five years and an unlikely event to reach that point. And within an instant, my life had changed.

Sitting in my room that night just before it was time to close things out for the day, I took out the journal they had given me on the very first day. On the nightstand, I had a pencil. It was one of those short miniature golf pencils. That is all that they gave us to write with. Self-harm prevention—these people thought of everything. We were encouraged to write in our journal every night. This was the first time I did. It would also be the last. I only needed one entry, anyway. It said it all.

After one week in the mental healthcare facility, I was sent to a conference room. The lead psychiatrist at the Highlands and others on his team were sitting around the table waiting for me. I sat down, and they began asking me a bunch of questions. They were evaluating me to decide whether or not I was well enough to be released. The entire meeting probably lasted thirty minutes or so. The lead psychiatrist gave me the all-clear.

My final obligation to be released from the Highlands was to have a "safety plan" in place—one that had to be reviewed and signed off on by the counselor responsible for giving me the final green light. This was not optional. The safety plan consisted of a variety of things to keep my recovery on track.

There were two final requirements for my release. The first was to "step down" to the Highlands Partial Hospitalization Program (PHP). The PHP entailed two weeks of all-day coping classes, much like the ones in inpatient. The intent of the PHP was to serve as a transition back to regular day-to-day life. The additional requirement for my release was a promise to find a therapist and psychiatrist for ongoing care. I completed everything to the counselor's satisfaction, and a couple of hours later, I was led to the door leading out to the lobby. I heard a buzz. The lock was released, and there was Marie, waiting for me in the lobby.

29 | RECLAIMING MY DIGNITY? RESTORING MY POWER?

The only known antidote to fear is faith.
—Woodrow Kroll

Shortly after leaving the Highlands, I began the process of trying to get my life back on track. Returning to my job was not on the table. Aside from needing more time to continue the recovery process, Marie and I agreed that there was no point in going back to the position and the company that had been so problematic for me in the first place. From a financial perspective, we could only go so long with neither of us working, but I needed to get better, and Marie was intent on helping me do it.

The first order of business: Marie and I discussed how we were going to approach finding the right therapist for me. Before I left the

Highlands, Kaylie gave me the name and number of the therapist she went to and recommended that I go see her. Marie and I agreed that this would be a good starting point. My first visit with Kaylie's therapist was fine, but I did not feel any connection with her. I spoke with Marie about the visit, and we agreed that I should continue looking.

A friend of ours had mentioned that we might want to check with our church to see if they knew of any therapists that integrated faith into their practice. We both thought it was a good idea, so I stopped by the office at our church and asked. The person at the desk had a brochure of a therapist they often referred people to, so I took it home with me, read through it and decided to go ahead and schedule an appointment.

Sarah had a home office in the foothills of Colorado. The drive there took about thirty minutes, just enough to clear my head but not so long that it was an inconvenience. The closer I got to her home, the more scenic the drive became. Evergreens dotted the landscape, and it felt peaceful being so close to the mountains. By the time I arrived at Sarah's, I felt somewhat relaxed. I sat in her waiting room for just a few minutes before Sarah came out to greet me and led me back to her office.

Like the landscape around her home, Sarah's office was quiet and peaceful. The walls were made of wood paneling. Her desk was modest, with one of those attached bookcases that rose above it. She had a large office chair with a high vertical back and wheels. The color was light beige and blended in with the desk behind her. There was another similar chair across from her for clients, no wheels—very comfortable. Above that chair and to the upper right was a small window that allowed some sunlight to shine through. It was a small, cozy office, a relaxed setting that fit its purpose.

Sarah and I were about the same age, and we spent the next forty-five minutes getting to know one another. She was easy to talk to and had a calming effect on me. She described her approach to therapy as integrating practical techniques with spirituality. It all made sense to me, and I came away thinking Sarah was the right person to help me in my recovery process. I told Marie about the session, and she agreed that it would be worth giving Sarah a try. One week later, the sessions began.

Sarah always started our session with a look back on how things went over the past week, much like the daily emotional check-in at the inpatient unit. I would tell her about my highs and lows along with anything else of significance that came to mind. From there we would transition to the work at hand. At first, that meant helping me continue to remain stable as I transitioned back into day-to-day life after the Highlands. Along with that, she focused on helping me handle the ups and downs of trying to find the right job—one that I was capable of performing without becoming overwhelmed and falling back into deep despair.

Sarah continued the work I began at the Highlands, reinforcing the coping skills I had learned there and teaching me new ones based on spirituality. Sarah is a person of deep faith, which was reassuring to me. These spirituality skills became not only a part of my healing, but also a set of weapons in my battle against the enemy. She called it spiritual warfare—calling on Christ to vanquish depression or, put another way, to stop the lies that my thoughts keep telling me, thereby rendering depression powerless.

No matter what a person believes, I learned from Sarah that connecting with whatever spirituality resonates with you is a must for finding the hidden strength that is bigger and more powerful than you and your challenges.

Above and beyond the coping skills, Sarah had an almost insurmountable task—to help me make sense of why I ended up at the Highlands at fifty-one years old. Her conviction was that while depression was at the center of the problem, there had to be things that happened throughout my life that exacerbated it and were left unresolved. These needed to be addressed. She was right—I just had to be convinced of it.

So as time went by and I gradually started to get my life back on track, I was ready to try something totally different. A giant leap of faith would be required for this one. I had gone through the work of telling Sarah about the events of the past that I thought could have worsened the depression. Some of these I have described to you, but there were more. And in my sessions I would recall one after another as the memories came back to me. From my perspective, they were always there, but over the years I had just forgotten about them. It was only natural for one to pop up now and then as we talked about my life experiences.

But Sarah had a different explanation. She said that I had buried the events in my subconscious to avoid the pain associated with them. She told me that my past was filled with a series of traumatic events, and even if I ever found an antidepressant that worked for me, I would never be completely healed until they were addressed. They had to be confronted and put to rest. I was skeptical. But that was not all: Sarah went a step further, telling me that the little boy who was bullied at a very early age and never felt safe was still inside me. And there was more. To rid myself of the scared, anxious, and beaten-down boy who still resided in me, I would have to go back to the difficult times in the past as my "adult self." That would be the path, she said, to "reclaiming my dignity" and "restoring my power."

At that point, she started to lose me. Return to the past as my adult self? I didn't think so—I couldn't even fully understand what that meant. This was the stuff of made-for-TV fiction—a bridge too far. I resisted. She persisted. Things were going nowhere for a long time. I was not taking my doctor's advice and had no interest in caving. But more than two years went by, and I couldn't shake the depression. I still had massive lows. Something had to give: I did. The time travel would begin.

Sarah started by asking me to think of a place where I felt safe growing up. I couldn't think of one. The closest I could get to such a place was when I would visit Nana. But her apartment was more of a place to relax, to be with somebody who made me feel at ease and good about myself. I never thought of it as a place to go to for safety. As I racked my brain to find a safe place, I started thinking about why it was so difficult for me. And then my thoughts turned to my "best friend" Mitch. I could never get away from his reach growing up. It got to the point where even when he was not present, the thought of when he would return never left my mind. He had gotten inside my head. He never left.

I remembered the many Saturday mornings when I would be sound asleep in my bedroom. Then suddenly, there was somebody shaking my whole body, and I would look up, half asleep. And there he was, standing over me laughing. With glee. He thought it was the funniest thing in the world. To me, it was mean-spirited. Which it was—and he knew it. Which is why it brought him so much pleasure. Somewhere, deep down inside of me, I wanted to tell Mitch:

"What the hell are you doing? And stop with that hideous laugh. It's not funny."

But I knew that would have resulted in his signature look of intimidation combined with his threatening voice:

"What's your problem, Slow? You better be careful. You're such a wimp."

That was his nickname for me: "Slow."

Mitch started calling me "Slow" when I was in middle school. He used to get a kick out of playing practical jokes on me. They were almost always demeaning, apparently intended to harass me. And time and time again, I would fall for them. Eventually, he started telling everybody how gullible I was. Actually, I just didn't think the way he did. Why would a friend, let alone your best friend, want to demean you constantly? It simply never occurred to me.

Yes, I was aware that being around Mitch was not easy, but we did a lot of things together, and I got lulled into thinking his personality and behavior, while rough, were not that big of a deal. It became almost normal to me in a sick way.

Part of that thinking was probably because none of the adults in my life ever made anything of it. They played a role in normalizing it. He would often call me "Slow," sometimes around family and other times around friends, and nobody ever said a word about it. Looking back, I think they were scared of him, too. You just never knew when Mitch was going to erupt with rage and what would happen if he did. Everybody seemed to manage to steer clear of it. I got caught in it. And the more he treated me like that, the more beaten-down I became. My self-esteem went south, and I became increasingly compliant until eventually, there was no fight left in me. I couldn't turn it around. Whatever ability I once had had to bounce back vanished.

If, by chance, you are thinking to yourself right now: "Bobby's starting to sound like he's playing the victim card," I can assure you that is not the case. I am merely retelling the reality of what my relationship with Mitch was like. It is a part of how my depression gained strength. Negative outside influences matter. They are important for anybody to be sensitive to, but for somebody who is suffering from depression, the implications of failing to recognize them are enormous. Depression is a devastating disease to begin with. There is no reason to give it fuel. This is not about victimhood—it is about understanding one of the ways a person's depression can be triggered or aggravated.

In any case, back to how "Slow" came to be. Along with the gullibility, Mitch always made me feel on guard. It was draining being in his presence. He had a way of beating me down psychologically. I was already exhausted from depression, and being around him did not help. I had to be cautious about what I said and how I said it out of fear of his explosive anger. You just never knew for sure what would set him off. I became weak.

So, there you have it: gullible, cautious, and weak. Mitch picked up on all of it and created his term of endearment: "Slow." What a genius.

Then, there were the intermittent calls. I could hear him through the phone:

"Where's Bobby, Mrs. Straus?"

He would say it with a voice that said, this is not a question. My mom would tell me Mitch was on the phone. I would ask her to say that I wasn't home. Not every time, but often. Sometimes I just desperately wanted to be left alone. I always wanted to rest, to sleep. My mom would tell me:

"Don't give me that. It's your best friend, Mitch. Now pick up the phone."

I had no choice, or at least that is what I came to accept. And being on the phone with him was nerve-racking. One would think that disagreeing with Mitch while on the phone would make you feel a little safer. Not the case. If I dared to try and stick up for myself, Mitch had a way of managing that quite effectively. He would raise his voice, and in a threatening tone with an undercurrent of rage, he would say:

"I wish I could put my fist through the phone and punch you in the fuckin' face."

I was never out of his reach.

Now, coming full-circle to the search for a safe place, over the course of my therapy sessions with Sarah, I was finally able to identify one. But I will save that for later. At this point, I was having trouble thinking of one. But we needed to move forward, so I decided on a place that I felt fairly confident would suffice. Our work could officially begin.

And the first session was a journey back to the very beginning—the playground when I was six years old. Sarah told me I had to go back there as my "adult self" and take that little boy still inside me out of harm's way. Not sure how that was going to happen, but Sarah assured me that this was the way back to "reclaiming my dignity" and "restoring my power." She would say this often over the next twelve months or so. And Sarah would also say that she would be there with me, guiding me through the process every step of the way.

It was time.

30 | THE DAM BREAKS

I could feel the tears brimming and sloshing in me
like water in a glass that is unsteady and too full.

—Sylvia Plath

The session begins, and I am sitting in my chair. As usual, the room is quiet and peaceful. Sarah tells me to close my eyes. She pauses for a few seconds. Her voice is calm and reassuring as she begins:

"Bobby—just relax. Let all the stress go. Take deep, slow breaths."

Then there is a brief pause, and she asks me if I am starting to feel relaxed. I let her know I am—my eyes still shut—and then she tells me to relax from my head to my neck, to my shoulders and arms, pausing for a while at each point.

"Just relax. Let all the stress fall off of you. Continue breathing deeply."

And she continues this pattern down my body.

By the time she is done, any stress and anxiety that I carried into our appointment are gone. I have drifted away from my surroundings, and my mind is clear of any thoughts I had before I shut my eyes. I have reached a state of complete relaxation. The time has come to recall the memory.

"Bobby, try and think back to that time on the playground. I need you to try and recall it."

I say nothing. My mind is searching for the memory.

"Bobby, Bobby—what's going on?"

As I become more and more focused on finding my way back to that playground, I become increasingly detached from everything around me. As crazy as it may sound, the search for that playground is starting to become real.

"I'm still trying to recall the memory."

After some time—how much, I am not exactly sure—I do.

"I'm there."

"What do you see, Bobby?"

"There are two teachers. They're having a conversation. I see the sandbox that I used to play in, and there are kids having fun. The hopscotch chalkboard on the pavement is right next to it. I see more children lined up to take their turn." I pause, not sure what to do.

"Do you see the slide?"

"No. There are the swings. I used to love those."

I am now scanning the whole playground, searching for the slide. I am immersed in the situation.

"What else do you see, Bobby?" I hear Sarah, but her voice is becoming distant, secondary to where I am and what I am looking for.

"Bobby? Where are you, Bobby?"

I do not respond.

"Bobby?"

I was now detached, completely caught up in the memory.

Whatever she was saying was now faint, background noise. I was back in a danger zone, focused on recalling that slide, drifting away from my connection to Sarah and the chair I was sitting in.

While the objective of the therapy is to become fully engaged in the memory, it has to be balanced with maintaining a connection to Sarah. She is my guide, a voice leading me through the process of recalling a traumatic event, confronting it, conquering the psychological grip it holds on me, and then gradually bringing me out of it. If I become disengaged from her, there will be nobody to help me if things start going wrong. Put another way, if I start to become overwhelmed as I confront the past, the adult mindset could weaken and that child still within me could reemerge. The likely outcome would be that the trauma happens all over again. It would be a major setback, potentially a total disaster.

Yes, I know what you are thinking, Sarah could intervene at any point. Okay, but when? Who knows the pace of time within which any part of a memory can play out? It would always be a judgment call, and nobody's perfect.

That's why there has to be a Plan B. This is where my safe place comes into the picture. At any moment, if I feel I am on the brink of getting overwhelmed by the trauma, Plan B has to kick in. I have to be able to call upon it without even thinking. The only way to ensure that? Practice. It begins with establishing the place of safety.

I come up with the best safe place that I can think of at that point in time. It was a stretch, but we go with it. It was a room I stayed in for a couple of nights in a beautiful hotel tucked away in a serene area of upstate New York, in Saratoga Springs. I knew it well because it was not far from where I spent my freshman year in college. My two-night stay at the hotel took place just after I left the bond firm in Manhattan. At that time, I wanted to get away from everything. I needed a place to clear my head as I thought about what would be next in life. As it turned out, what would be next in life was my move to Albuquerque, New Mexico.

With my safe place selected, Sarah begins the conditioning process. She takes me through the steady sequence of getting me into a completely relaxed state. Next, she asks me to recall that hotel in Saratoga Springs. I think back to that time and place, and I can remember it. My eyes remain shut, and I am locked in on the beautiful landscape surrounding the grand hotel. I hear Sarah's voice, and she guides me through the front entrance into the lobby and up the stairs to the room, having me describe what I see every step of the way. Once in the room, she has me tell her everything I can about what I see inside of it. I look through the room, trying to remember whatever I can about it, and as I describe to Sarah everything I see, I become immersed in the memory.

When I finish, I go over to the bed and sit at the end of it. I take in the peacefulness of where I am, even feeling the breeze coming through the window. It has all become real. The first round of conditioning is now complete. There will be more to come to reach the point where I will be able to go to this room instantaneously. It will become my escape hatch, the means of removing myself from a traumatic memory before it overtakes me for a second time. But Plan B needs time to become firmly established. My sense of peace at this moment is a false one. The escape hatch is not yet ready for liftoff, and I am now in unchartered territory.

Gradually, as I am sitting on the bed, totally at ease, my mind starts to wander. I begin to think about my time living in New York City while I was working at the bond firm. I can see the neighborhood where I lived, the restaurants I got takeout from for dinner every night after work. I am standing on the sidewalk, my apartment building not too far away. I see the stairs leading down to the subway I took to work every morning. I don't even know if that was close to where I was standing, but that image came to mind. It was not a pleasant one. And that is when my mind started to drift. I was still sitting on the bed in that peaceful room in Saratoga Springs, but any sense of it was gone.

And then, without a hint of transition, I find myself sitting at that bond desk next to Henry amidst the sea of brokers and traders. I remember the chaotic environment, and I feel the high stress of being in it. And, as for the escape hatch? Without the room, there is no escape hatch. I am on my own and in the trauma before Sarah even realizes it. Instantaneously, Henry is standing up, his finger pointed at me, his face red with anger. I can feel his resentment toward me. How could somebody as stupid as me be sitting at that desk next to him? He raises his voice and starts berating me. It is all happening again. It feels like an ambush. Everything around me gets louder, including Henry's voice. It all starts playing out in slow motion. I don't know what to do—it's all too much to handle. No way out. And that is when it happens. Rising up from the depths of the dark ocean waters in the midst of a storm, the tidal wave of depression comes roaring toward me. It is a wall of fury. I hate that feeling.

I hear Sarah's voice and, at the same time, mine. I remember little about what I am saying other than snippets about New York City and the bond desk and Henry yelling at me.

Sarah's voice starts to become louder. I know she is trying to pull me out of the state I am in.

And then it happens, like a dam breaking after decades of holding back steadily rising water—the tears come gushing out of my eyes. My sadness is uncontrollable. Sarah's voice is louder and stronger. She is trying to break the cycle I am in and settle me down. She finally did—it took about twenty minutes.

I was exhausted and drained, but that experience marked the beginning of my healing. It kick-started what had to happen—the releasing of the sadness and pain that had been denied for far too long, eating me alive every step of the way.

In the months ahead, there will be plenty more to come. I would never have thought Henry would end up being the catalyst for my road to recovery. I guess I should thank him. No, I'll pass.

31 | AT LONG LAST, REST

Come to me, all who are weary and
heavy-laden, and I will give you rest.

—Matthew 11:28

Something tells me that at this point, you may be thinking this is all ridiculous, not believable. And, before I started this form of therapy, I would have agreed with you. In fact, I did agree with you. But we would all be wrong. This type of treatment exists. It is time-tested, and many people experience great benefit from it.

Now, back to where I was. I believe there was a large part of me that did not want to go back to that slide. Who the hell would? But there I was, scanning the playground in search of it.

"Tell me what is going on, Bobby." Sarah's voice had a hint of concern in it.

I said nothing, staring at some scattered pine trees that I seemed to remember. I knew the slide was not far from them, and I could feel my heart beating faster. The slide began to come into view.

"I see it. I see the slide."

Sarah's voice is gone.

"Oh, jeez." There is a sense of disbelief and sadness in my voice as that little boy at the bottom of the slide comes into view. How could all of this have really happened?

But there he is, lying on his side in a ball in the dirt, knees pressed against his stomach, elbows against each knee. His forearms extend over his chest with his hands covering his face, holding the top of his head, which is turned inward, chin pressed against the bottom of his neck. I can see him—that skinny little boy with red hair, and I remember that yellow-brown long-sleeved shirt and brown corduroy pants. He is trying the best he can to protect himself from the kicking coming at him from all sides, up and down his body, and the fists landing against his hands and head—he is just lying there, completely helpless. I remember thinking, "Please, just let it be over." He needs help, but there is nobody watching. Why couldn't they have just seen me?

"Bobby, tell me what is happening." Sarah's voice is still with me.

"I'm there again," I tell her.

And then, instinctively, I step into the memory. That little boy needs help. I start running toward the slide, yelling at the boys: "Get off of him!" They run off as I near the little boy. I reach him and kneel. He is shaking and does not move.

"Hey, I'm here to help you," I say in a soft voice. He does not respond.

"Bobby—they are gone. It's over." My voice is still quiet, trying to be reassuring. I see him spread his fingers slightly, looking through them.

"It's okay. I came to get you away from all of this."

I stay where I am, just giving him time to realize he is now safe. Slowly, he gathers just enough courage to take his hands away from his face. He is beginning to realize that I want to help him. As he looks at me, I reach out for him to take my hand. He does. I help him up.

"It's over, Bobby. I am not going to let anybody hurt you anymore. Okay?"

"Okay," he replies, still shaking but more trusting. Still holding his hand, I begin walking him off the playground.

Sarah has been listening all the while, and then I hear her voice again.

"Bobby, where are you now?"

"I'm walking away from the playground with the little boy."

"Okay, where are you going?"

"Church." About a half a mile away from the elementary school was the church where I was baptized.

Once we are safely away from the playground, I kneel again, holding each of the little boy's hands, and look at him. He was still shaking, but he had calmed down quite a bit and looked back at me.

"We are going to leave now. Are you ready?" He nodded his head in agreement, his eyes red from all the crying. Taking him in my arms, I hugged him. "Let's go."

When we get to the church, I lead the little boy to a pew toward the front and sit down with him to my left. I put my left arm around his back, my hand taking hold of his upper arm. He leans in toward me and rests his head on my shoulder. His shaking is gone. At that moment, I feel a sense of calm taking over. It is so peaceful and quiet sitting there with him. I hear Sarah's voice again.

"Bobby, how are you doing?"

"I'm starting to feel a little better." My voice is slightly more than a whisper as I remain very much within the memory.

I take my right arm and extend it over his chest, taking hold of his left upper arm and pulling him in closer, holding him tighter. I lean in toward him and tilt my head left, lowering it gently until my temple lands softly against the top of his head. My eyes well up with tears. I hear him sigh. It is the kind of sigh that is full of relief. I shut my eyes, and tears run down my cheeks. That, I thought, is what it must be like to feel safe. I never want to let it go. Finally, I am resting.

After some time, how long I am not sure, I hear Sarah's voice: "Bobby, are you ready?"

"Yes," I say faintly, as if awakening from a deep sleep.

"I want you to take whatever time you need, and then slowly open your eyes."

Within a few minutes, I gradually open my eyes. And there is Sarah, sitting calmly in her chair, waiting patiently for me to find my way back to the present. Blinking, I look up at her. I feel calm.

"Are you with me, Bobby?"

"Yes." I had come full-circle.

"Bobby," she said, "when you get home tonight, I want you to drink a lot of water and get sleep. You are going to feel drained, and that is normal. Make sure you rest."

And that was it. What was likely the event, or certainly a part of an early series of childhood events, that triggered a life of depression, was laid to rest. I was on my way back home.

Over the next year, I returned to the events in my life that we had identified as traumatic, one-by-one, going back to them and changing the outcomes. And Sarah was right: with each session, I was reclaiming a little piece of my dignity. At the same time, my power was being restored. It seemed more gradual, but it was happening. I was becoming stronger, more confident.

With time, it became apparent that the therapy was having a

dramatic positive impact on me. Sarah was changing my life. No—she was giving it back to me.

32 | GOODBYE, POLAR

To sit with a dog on a hillside on a glorious
afternoon is to be back in Eden, where doing
nothing was not boring—it was peace.
—Milan Kundera

In the midst of the intense therapy sessions with Sarah, Polar's health went into a steady decline, and I could feel the sadness building throughout our family as he became sicker. What would happen to us when he was gone? He was, after all, the Great Connector. Polar had been with Marie every day, her shadow throughout the house. As she struggled with taking care of Jack while I was working long hours and then collapsing at home after work and on weekends, Polar never left her side. Inasmuch as he was able to do the impossible and connect me to the world, he was also a reliable, reassuring presence for Marie. A major support system.

And then there was Jack. Polar loved to be with Jack, and Jack was crazy about Polar. He looked out for Polar like one would hope a big brother would watch out for their younger brother.

Every Fourth of July we would light off fireworks with our neighbors in the cul-de-sac. I would take Polar out on his leash so he could be a part of it. Fireworks did not bother him, and he would never pass up an opportunity to be around people, a personality trait that he and Jack had in common.

Throughout the night, Jack would intermittently look over at me and say: "Make sure Polar doesn't get too close to the fireworks." He said it with a mixture of authority and caring—very sweet. I would reassure Jack that I had it under control, and off he would go to play with the neighborhood kids as we all enjoyed the celebration together.

Every once in a while, though, I would see Jack stop playing for a few seconds and look back over at Polar again to make double and triple sure he remained on the perimeter, away from the fireworks. Jack took nothing for granted. As long as he was around, Polar was going to be safe.

The last July 4th we would celebrate with Polar was in 2015. He was just a few months away from his tenth birthday, and it was becoming increasingly apparent that Polar's health was declining. None of us said anything about it, but we could all feel it. In the late spring of that year, the seriousness of Polar's condition became quite clear to me when I went to take him for one of our walks around the block. We both loved to take walks together—it was therapeutic for me, and Polar was always up for saying hello to his many fans. To be clear, Polar never had any interest in long hikes, but he was always up for a leisurely stroll together. I put his leash on, and Polar followed me out the laundry room door into the garage. As always, he waited patiently for the garage door to open and then followed me out to the driveway.

We got to about the middle of the driveway when Polar came to a sudden, abrupt halt and sat down. At first, I thought he was pausing to look around the cul-de-sac, so I paused for a few seconds before giving a slight tug on the leash to start our walk again. He did not move. I looked down at him. He looked up at me, sitting there in his trademark kickstand position. He would not budge. A few seconds more and another gentle tug on his leash, this time with words of encouragement: "Come on, buddy, let's go." Nothing. He was not going anywhere. He seemed happy enough sitting out on the driveway, so I stayed there with him for about ten minutes before turning around to go back inside. As I started to walk towards the garage, I barely had to tug on Polar's leash, as he got up and followed me straight back into the house. He would never take a stroll around the neighborhood again.

Polar had a heart murmur that was quiet, but audible when he was very young. Our vet, Dr. Timothy O'Brien, informed us about the heart problem—mitral valve disease (MVD)—that virtually all Cavaliers develop at some point in their lives. Dr. O'Brien gave Marie and I comfort that the murmur was nothing to be alarmed about at that point, and that he would monitor it throughout Polar's life.

Dr. O'Brien had been our vet for a long time, and we trusted that Polar was in good hands, which he undoubtedly was. Neither of us felt a pressing need to run to the internet and research MVD. I am glad we didn't. It spared us years of worry over what was to inevitably come.

In the late spring of 2015, it became painfully apparent to me that Polar was getting closer to the tipping point. I was not prepared for it and tried to rationalize it as just an off day. The only problem was that when it came to a walk around the neighborhood, Polar did not have off days. Looking back, that moment marked the beginning of my denial. The thought of losing Polar was more than I could bear. So, I didn't think it—my self-destructive coping strategy kicking in once again. But I have to cut myself a break on this one. It had only been about six months since my release from the Highlands, and I needed time to try and get a semblance of a life back. There wouldn't be one without Polar in it.

In the final few months of Polar's life, his health went into a steep decline. He was no longer able to rest comfortably for extended periods, lying down for a few minutes on his stomach, then sitting up for a few more. Intermittently he would change positions and lie on his side. He would still shadow Marie and, without fail, be sitting in his kickstand position ready to make the sprint toward me when I got home from work every night.

But the inability to rest comfortably for longer periods was exacting a heavy toll on Polar. The medications that Dr. O'Brien had prescribed more than a year ago had been quite effective in extending his quality of life, but as Dr. O'Brien had told us to prepare for, at some point the meds would not be enough to stem the tide of the disease's progression. That point had arrived. Dr. O'Brien advised us to stop—there were no more drugs available to help Polar. Corrective surgery was never an option. There was simply no surgical procedure available to fix or replace the faulty valve. He did not give Polar much time.

In the final month of Polar's life, he would lie on his side against the kitchen door leading out to the back patio. I am not sure why he started to do this, but my hunch is that he wanted to be close to the back patio where he spent many days and evenings sitting outside and taking a whiff of the breeze. I think it was just a peaceful place for him, and he needed that in his final days. I knew time was running out for my best friend, and I did not want him to be alone. And I did not want to be alone, either. So, when Jack and Marie were asleep, late at night, I would quietly get out of bed and walk down the stairs and into the kitchen to be with him. Polar was almost always awake, changing positions and trying to get comfortable for as long as he could. I would sit down next to him on the floor and begin to pet him softly.

I always remember when he would come into my room at night in the final days of my job at the consulting firm. I would be lying down on my back in the evening, staring up at the ceiling, trying to get some rest and feel a moment of relief. But that time had long since passed. I was going downhill at an increasingly rapid pace but did not realize what was to come. Polar would jump onto the bed and lie east-west across my chest. I would pet him, starting on the top of his head and finishing toward the end of his back, repeating the pattern as he continued to lie in that position, all the while telling him my troubles. I could feel his heart beating against my chest. Polar would typically last for about ten minutes lying down across my chest before he was unable to stay in that position. Then, without warning, off he would go. But for that short time every night, Polar gave me the gift of peace in my otherwise constant state of despair.

Now, it was my turn. As I sat next to Polar on the kitchen floor stroking him softly, I would tell him how much I loved him and that no matter what, we would always be together. I just tried to soothe him as much as I could. He would lie there listening for a while. Then, he would need to change positions, moving to a sitting position. At those times, I would kneel in front of him to get to his eye level and rest my forehead gently against his. We would be gazing straight into each other's eyes at a distance of just a few inches apart. At the same time, I would take my hands and gently hold either side of his head. I told him how much I wished he did not have to go. I could see the sadness in his eyes as I spoke to him. His eyes were expressive, and he had a unique ability to speak with them. Polar was ready. His declining health was getting the best of him.

After trying to reassure him for a while that I would always be by his side, I stepped away and then sat back down a few feet from him. My head went naturally down between my knees, and my arms wrapped around them to hold me steady. I cried. I knew he had to go, and the decision to let him find rest and tranquility was near. He had given me so much. He had given our family so much. My tears were mixed with feelings of thinking about the emptiness that would come after he was gone, and the fear of losing his incredible ability to connect me to the world.

It had been over a year since my stay at the Highlands. Life for my family and I was getting much better. Wondering whether or not I could maintain my connection to the world without Polar was scaring the hell out of me. That feeling, though, was a distant second to the pain and sadness of letting go.

In a last-ditch effort to prolong Polar's life while trying to improve the quality of it, Dr. O'Brien recommended a procedure to drain fluid that was now rapidly filling up inside of him. The buildup of fluid throughout his body was a natural part of the disease's progression. One of the veterinarians in Dr. O'Brien's practice was Dr. Meredith Bailey. She had been a part of Polar's care for a long time and was well-versed in this procedure. Dr. Bailey took the reins and performed the procedure on Polar. It immediately helped. When we parked the car in the garage and let Polar out, he went straight to the door leading into the laundry room and then came bounding into the kitchen like a hotshot. He was back! It was a miracle! His labored breathing was gone, as was his hacking cough. We could see the life beaming out of him just like the months before his medication stopped helping him. Marie, Jack, and I were hopeful and excited. Polar would be with us for months to come.

Our hopes were dashed within two weeks of the procedure. The fluid was building up again, and his symptoms returned. We spoke with Dr. Bailey about repeating the procedure. We had seen such a dramatic change in Polar after the first one, and thought maybe she could drain even more fluid out of him this time to extend his life even more. She agreed, and once again Polar responded. We thought perhaps the fluid would not build up as quickly this time. Of course, we were wrong. In less than a week, Polar was right back where he started, and within the next couple of days he had become extremely fatigued, his hacking cough gaining in frequency. We conferred with Dr. Bailey again—perhaps one more of her procedures to give us a little more time. She said it would not be fair to Polar. The fluid came back so quickly in the last procedure that another one was not going to help him. It was time to let go.

On March 30, 2016, we took Polar in to see Dr. Bailey. She told us it was coming dangerously close to the point at which the fluid that was now rapidly building up in his lungs would fill them up completely. If this happened, the fluid would drown him. It would be a horrible death. There was no way we were going to let that happen. We asked Dr. Bailey if she thought Polar would be okay for one more night with us. She felt he had another night but said to stay with him the whole night. If his hacking started to worsen, we should take him straight to the hospital to have him euthanized. There was a 24-hour veterinary hospital about three minutes from our home, so she felt comfortable letting us take Polar home for one more night.

That evening, Polar went into our laundry room and lay down on his side. We were all with him, watching him closely and supporting one another. Late that night, he started to hack. We got ready to rush him to the hospital. And then, all of a sudden, he got up and ran toward his spot in the kitchen—the one where he would sit in his kickstand position where he would be every night when I got home from work. We were relieved. None of us wanted his last moments to be in a sterile environment where he didn't know anyone. We fully realized there was a slight chance of that when we left Dr. Bailey earlier in the day, but she assured us that it was highly unlikely. If Dr. Bailey had said there was too much of a risk to get him through one more night, we would have let him go. Fortunately, Dr. Bailey was right, and early the next morning, we put Polar in the car and went to Dr. O'Brien's clinic together.

On this final day of March, snow was falling. The weather was dreary. We arrived at the parking lot of the clinic. Marie put Polar's leash on to take him into the clinic where Dr. Bailey would euthanize him. Marie wanted to be with Polar until the end. I desperately wanted to be there, too, but said nothing. Polar had been Marie's rock through incredibly difficult times. Day in and day out, he was always with her as she went about her day. Marie had also built a solid relationship with Dr. Bailey. She needed to be with Polar, and in the end, I wanted her to be with him, too.

So, I knelt to say my final goodbye to Polar. Holding him tightly, I told him how much I loved him as I rested my head gently against him. I did not want to ever let go, but it was time. Next, Jack said his good-bye. Tears were rolling down both of our faces as we watched Marie walk away with Polar. When they got about halfway to the entrance of the clinic, Polar looked back at Jack and I as he walked by Marie's side. His right ear flopped back as it had been so many times before. My mind took a snapshot of that moment, and it remains vivid in my memory. I hope it always does. March 31, 2016, was the saddest day of my life. By far.

A few days after we lost Polar, a card arrived in the mail. It was from Dr. O'Brien's clinic, and he and everybody in the clinic had signed it. The card contained a poem. As difficult as it was to be without Polar, the poem gave us all a sense of peace.

THE RAINBOW BRIDGE

Just this side of heaven is a place called Rainbow Bridge.

When an animal dies that has been especially close to someone here, that pet goes to Rainbow Bridge. There are meadows and hills for all of our special friends so they can run and play together. There is plenty of food, water, and sunshine, and our friends are warm and comfortable.

All the animals who had been ill and old are restored to health and vigor. Those who were hurt or maimed are made whole and strong again, just as we remember them in our dreams of days and times gone by. The animals are happy and content, except for one small thing; they each miss someone very special to them, who had to be left behind.

They all run and play together, but the day comes when one suddenly stops and looks into the distance. His bright eyes are intent. His eager body quivers. Suddenly he begins to run from the group, flying over the green grass, his legs carrying him faster and faster.

You have been spotted, and when you and your special friend finally meet, you cling together in joyous reunion, never to be parted again. The happy kisses rain upon your face; your hands again caress the beloved head, and you look once more into the trusting eyes of your pet, so long gone from your life but never absent from your heart.

Then you cross Rainbow Bridge together....
—Author unknown

33 | LIFE LESSONS FROM POLAR

I think dogs are the most amazing creatures;
they give unconditional love. For me,
they are the role model for being alive.

—Gilda Radner

In the days and weeks following Polar's death, there was an emptiness throughout our home and family. Over the years, Polar had become our shared beating heart. When his heart finally gave way, so did ours. But Marie and Jack had a bond so deep and so strong that together they were managing the loss. They never excluded me. I did that all on my own—always had, never by choice. Polar's death left the door wide open for the depression to sever whatever remaining connection I had to them. No surprise—out came the ax. I was on my own. No doubt, a joyous moment for the merciless disease.

Two months out from Polar's death, my grief was getting worse. It was wearing me down, and I did not know what to do with it. So, I did what had come naturally—wait it out. Eventually, it would subside. And, over a few weeks, no surprise, it didn't. I think the depth of sorrow I was experiencing had become so overwhelming that I just buried it. Old habits do die hard. But as Sarah had already taught me, nothing of that magnitude ever goes away—not on its own. Time for another lesson.

Sarah saw the grief every time I spoke about Polar, but every time she brought it up, I glossed over it. She needed to find a way to pull it out of me. And she did, with a little twist. Over several sessions, Sarah encouraged me to think about some of my memories of Polar and things he may have taught me. I was very reluctant; everything felt so raw. I could not bring myself to do it. So, she took a different approach, bringing up the idea of having me write a letter to Polar. In the worst way, I did not want to go there, but at each session, after she first suggested the idea of writing the letter, Sarah would ask me if I had done it. After three or four weeks of deny and delay, I relented. Late one night after work I grabbed a notebook and a pen, sat down at my desk, flipped to a blank page, and let my mind travel back to those special times with the Great Connector.

Dear Polar,

I remember when I would come home after work, open the garage door, and then walk through the doorway leading me into the laundry room. I would see you standing in your usual kickstand position looking back at me. Your eyes were happy and excited. And then I would call your name, and you would run toward me. I would kneel and welcome you into my arms, and for the next two or three minutes, all my troubles went away. Just you and me together. Your tail wagging and your head snuggled into my stomach. I would hold you close to me, and for those moments, I was not alone. I felt the warmth. We were together. Buddies welcoming each other home. I cherish those moments. Oh, how I wish you were there again when I opened the door after coming home from work. A few minutes of peace. My buddy and me. I wish you were still there. I miss you.

I remember when it was raining, and we would sit outside together— just outside the front door. Just me and my buddy taking in the rain. Same thing when it was snowing and on early evenings, anytime. And I remember all those times sitting on the back patio, sometimes just passing the time together, other times you would sit or lie down on the patio while I planted flowers. And then there were all those times when I would look out from the back-patio door watching you while you sniffed the breeze. You seemed so peaceful, so happy to be taking in the breeze. I remember you running in circles outside on our front yard out of nowhere. So joyful. You made me laugh. I wish you were here with me right now.

I never thought about what you taught me, but I am thinking about it now. The thing is, I never learned any of it. But as I look back, here are the things you gave me, and I hope I can honor you by living them:

LOVING BEING WITH PEOPLE: You were always so joyful when you were outside with me, and you saw all the neighbors. You would pull on the leash while your tail wagged like crazy until I relented and walked over to them. I always felt better after we visited, even though I did not want to.

EMBRACING THE MOMENT: You really did seem to enjoy the moment you were in. You were just as happy when we came back inside after visiting neighbors. It was onto the next thing, more fun to be had. It could have been just lying on the floor and resting peacefully—not a care in the world—or standing by your food bowl signaling any way you could that dinner would be served now. Every once in a while, you would bark if I wasn't responding. You made me get up. That was a good thing for me, even though I did not know it at the time.

KEEP MOVING: Keep moving. Lots more of life to enjoy. Get going. Then at the same time, you would lay down and rest. And you were peaceful. It never seemed that you were resting to get away from everything. You were resting because you were at peace. And when you woke up, you were energized, ready to go, onto the next adventure. Waking up was a great thing because you were ready to have more fun, not because you were worried about what was ahead. Off you went, let's go, plenty of things to explore, fun to be had.

NEVER AFRAID: You never seemed afraid of what was going to happen, you were just happy about the moment you were in. You were always looking for the next fun thing that was going to happen, not anything bad. In fact, I do not even think you ever thought anything terrible could happen. You never worried. You were carefree. Life was about possibilities, never fear. In terms of what the next moment would bring, I know you were never even aware or afraid. Fear did not exist. Only Joy.

Moment after moment, life was about living with joy. How much fun was next? A walk to soak up the outdoors—you weren't waiting for the walk to be over or sad that it would end. You just enjoyed the walk. When it was over, you weren't fearful of what was to come. The walk was fun now. What would be after it wasn't a thought. But whatever it would be, you weren't worried about it. You weren't thinking ahead what was to come, but if you were, I know it had to be about the next fun adventure, not drudgery.

Life was about play and great food and snacks, peaceful rest, and looking for ways to be a part of the party. Anything bad that might occur just wasn't a part of your thoughts. I know it, I saw it. You were looking for the next happy event. Fear, worry, sadness, hopelessness, concern about what anybody thought about you—these emotions and feelings did not exist in your life. Just the opposite: excitement, happiness, joy, embracing people, and doing things without any thought about what anyone might think about you. In fact, if you had any thought at all, I know it had to be:

"I love them. I want to be with them. I want to play with them. They have to love me back. I was happy; how could anyone think anything except how great I was? Unimaginable they could think otherwise; how great!"

Thank you for teaching me these things, Polar. I know you taught me so much more. I will write them down as they come to me. I miss you, Polar, but I remember you. I want to live the way I know you were teaching me to. And I know the more I live like everything you were teaching me to, the closer we will be together.

I probably wrote that letter in twenty minutes. Once I got started, the memories just came gushing out. I could not get the words on paper fast enough. Yes, tears were rolling down my cheeks; a few landed on the paper. I was letting go of grief—just what Sarah wanted. My healing had begun.

34 | THE GREAT PROTECTOR

Dogs come into our lives to teach us about love and loyalty.
They depart to teach us about loss. A new dog never
replaces an old dog; it merely expands the heart.
—Erica Jong

It was probably less than two months after we lost Polar that I first spoke to Marie about getting another dog. She was dead set against it, saying she was looking forward to not having to worry about the responsibilities of taking care of another dog. She was ready to move on. Jack was open to the idea, but wanted us to wait six months before deciding out of "respect for Polar." Smart kid. I understood both points of view—but for me, the pain of knowing we would lose another dog in our lifetimes was sad, but the sadness of not getting another one was worse, and I was in no condition to wait six months.

Polar was the first line of defense against my depression, my connection to the world. No dog could ever replace him, but all dogs are special spirits with tremendous therapeutic benefits. Trying to manage my depression without a dog would be like trying to keep diabetes under control without insulin—not an option. I would go it alone. No discussion. Surely, once I got a puppy, Marie would instantly fall in love with it. How could she resist? It was a lay-up. No, it was an impulsive, depression-driven decision. A massive mistake. An earthquake, 10.0 on the Richter scale. As it turned out, Marie could resist pretty damn well!

So off I went, throwing myself into an exhaustive search to find just the right breed. Another Cavalier King Charles Spaniel was off the table—there would never be another Polar. Over the next five months, I read about, identified, and visited all types of breeds that I thought would be ideal in helping me to manage my depression and also be a great family dog.

I finally consulted with a trainer who specialized in training service dogs. She highly recommended that I get a Goldendoodle. So, I visited some local breeders to learn more about them and see some of their dogs. I loved them: they were playful, smart, fun, loving, and had a strong desire to be around people. They are great companion and family dogs. The breed was everything I had read and heard about them. They did not shed, which I knew would be important to Marie, and they weren't too big, also something that I knew was key for Marie.

It was clear why the trainer recommended a Goldendoodle. It would be an excellent dog for providing me the therapeutic benefits that were a must and the type of dog that was likely to engage me with people. But in the end, something was missing from the breed, so I turned it down.

Somewhere along the way of my search, I concluded that, given my life history, a dog that would help to provide me with a sense of safety was paramount. Ideally, that meant a dog that had all the qualities of a Goldendoodle but was also bigger, more powerful, and had a strong, protective streak with an instinct about when to turn it on. Finding a breed like this was a tall order—back to the drawing board.

After about three months, I came across a breed I was not familiar with: the Newfoundland. From everything I had read about them, it seemed like this dog would be perfect for me. I went to visit a breeder and was immediately awestruck. I had heard them described as gentle giants who had a protective streak and were known for their ability to instinctively rescue people who were drowning. Very impressive. My search was over: the Newfoundland was the one. That feeling lasted about two minutes. A Newfoundland could easily weigh 150 pounds. They shed a lot and are known for slobbering. Getting a dog without my wife on board was problematic enough—even during my depression meltdown, I knew getting a Newfoundland was marriage-ending material. Back to square one.

I spoke with my trainer about the Newfoundland, and she had an idea—a Newfoundland-Standard Poodle mix, also known as a Newfydoodle or Newfypoo. The breed was known to have the great personality traits of both of the breeds. They were not as large as a Newfoundland, although still big, weighing typically ninety to one-hundred pounds, and without shedding and slobbering. I remember the trainer saying, in a Zen way: "I feel this is the right breed for you." I knew Marie would not be thrilled with the size, but with the shedding and drooling out of the equation, I figured it could work.

On February 18, 2017, I boarded a Spirit Airlines plane and

traveled to the Newfypoo Zoo in Adrian, Michigan, to pick up the puppy who at first was called Red because that was the color of the ribbon he wore. We flew back to Colorado that day with Red resting in a carrier at my feet on the plane ride home. I thought he would get some sleep on the plane, but he looked up at me almost the entire flight. It was the beginning of a bond between us that, over the past three years, has become so strong it is hard for me to understand—no need to try, just blessed to have him in my life.

When I got home with Red, it seemed like things might go better than I had anticipated. Hard to resist a puppy. And although Marie was unhappy with what I had done, it seemed as though Red's dazzling looks and personality, along with his puppy breath, might rule the day. Marie ended up picking out the name—Jasper. Eventually, she started calling him Jazz. The nickname stuck. Pretty good for somebody who did not want the dog in the first place.

I was glad Marie came up with the name and nickname. I thought it might help build a connection. Not quite that easy, but she did take note of what she called his "kind" eyes. I hadn't noticed it until Marie pointed it out, but I felt it from the start. They match his calm, loving personality along with his playful, comedic side.

But even as Marie seemed to be feeling better about having Jasper around, she remained careful to keep her distance, wanting to avoid getting too close to him. I understood why, but held out hope that over time, he would win her over. And over the first few months, it seemed like he was making progress. But then one afternoon, she opened the back door leading out to the patio. Jazz was outside, and she wanted him to come in. As he came running toward the door, he had a prize with him—a dead squirrel. And that was it—all south from there. I couldn't blame her; it was not the type of thing you would ever have caught Polar doing. Needless to say, the greeting I got was not pretty when I returned home from work. It was a setback of epic proportions. Then when he started shedding, as not advertised, it was game over. Six months later and Marie maintained her distance from Jasper and resented me. I understood and knew she had every reason to feel that way. Still, I hoped she could someday forgive me for my rash decision.

One year later, no progress. Marie was steadfast in not allowing herself to get close to Jasper, although her resentment toward me had softened; she is an incredibly forgiving person. In the meantime, Jack, who wanted little to do with Jasper early on, had come to enjoy having him around. But Jack, like Marie, seemed hesitant to allow himself to build a bond with Jasper. Over the next six months, though, Jasper's protective streak started to emerge, and Marie and Jack began to feel safer with him in our home. It was Jasper's protective nature that became his breakthrough character trait, paving the way for him to break open their hearts.

So how does Jasper's fiercely protective streak emerge from those kind eyes and calm, loving, peaceful demeanor? It comes about when he senses a threat on the horizon. The moment Jasper catches the first whiff of danger anywhere near me, as well as Marie and Jack, his presence and demeanor will change dramatically. When his alarm sounds, a sudden ear-shattering bark erupts. Then, one after another after another, the barking builds momentum. If he senses the threat is getting closer, a low rolling growl joins the barking. Jasper takes on a larger, menacing appearance. And then, if the danger seems imminent, he goes full-blown red alert. The barking and growling explode, and then a wolf-like howl reverberates through both. When these sounds come together, the explosiveness is mind-blowing. Under normal conditions, he is peaceful and happy, providing a feeling of complete calm and comfort. But, when he senses danger approaching, he can unleash a fury that nobody in their right mind would go near.

Jasper became a reassuring presence in my life, my faithful buddy. He comforted me like nobody else could from the waves of sadness that continued to come and go without warning. My life raft. And more than just his calming influence on my life, Jasper's playful spirit and fun-loving antics became a shared source of joy and laughter for Marie, Jack, and I. He was a source of safety for our family. Our Guardian. Truly, the Great Protector.

It is a Monday evening and I arrive home after another stressful day. I am exhausted. As usual, Jasper is in the laundry room waiting for me to walk in through the garage door. I am ready for the attack, and he does not disappoint. He jumps up, takes his massive paw and hits me on my chest. He is a giant. Then again, he takes a swing at me with his other paw. One after another, he swipes at me with his paws before I push my body into his, just hard enough to stop his rhythm and throw him off-kilter.

He falls back but lands on his front paws and steadies himself. Then, he stares back at me and starts growling, showing his big sharp teeth. His message is simple: "You have made a huge mistake and are about to pay for it." If somebody saw what was happening, they would likely have thought I was in grave danger. But that could not be further from the truth. It is all just beginning of our nightly ritual, and it does not end in the laundry room.

Next, like clockwork, Jazz turns around and starts heading toward the kitchen, taking a quick glance back to make sure I am chasing him. With very few exceptions, I do. Once he confirms that I am right behind him, he reaches the open space between our kitchen and family room and gets in position to teach me a lesson. He is ready for the one-to two-minute free-for-all.

And so it begins—the paw swings come at me harder and faster. The growling becomes louder and more intense. If I move in to try to push him away, Jazz takes the growling up a few decibels and adds a frenzied look as he snatches my forearm with his mouth and then quickly lets go of it. It only gets more out of control from there. Marie is usually nearby, standing in the kitchen shaking her head at us and waiting for it all to end. I am home. Whatever worries I brought with me are diminished, sometimes even gone.

But, as it turns out, this evening is one of those exceptions. I don't follow through and engage. I am wiped out and feeling down. What can I say? It's a Monday. When Jasper realizes I am not coming after him, he makes his way to his bed, lies down on his stomach, crosses his legs in front of him—his signature position—and locks his eyes on me.

I feel like I should try to shake off the desire to lay down and rest in our bedroom. I know it's not good for me. Marie can see that I'm extra tired and encourages me to take it easy: "Sometimes your body just needs rest, Bobby." I am not hard to convince. But instead of going upstairs and being alone, I figure I should at least sit down on the couch in our family room, which can be seen from the kitchen. Maybe if I just sit down for a half an hour and watch a little television, I'll feel better.

Not so fast. Just as I settle-in, I hear the pitter-patter of Jasper trotting along on the wood floor. He stops in front of me and looks up. I know the look—he wants to go outside. It is not a request. There is a door in our kitchen that leads right out to the back patio, and he makes his way toward it. His strides are purposeful. Then he pauses, looking back to make sure I understand the situation.

Jazz has switched to Plan B. I know the drill. He is not playing games—out the door we go. Within a matter of seconds, he is in the yard and sifting through his sticks. He has a whole pile full of them—small, medium, and large. After a brief inspection—this is serious business—he snatches one up with his mouth and turns toward me. Jasper is ready for me to chase him around the yard and try to grab the stick from him. One of his favorite activities.

But I just want to sit down on the patio and take in the cool, crisp autumn air. Hopefully, he will get the picture and just settle in on the grass and start grinding down his stick. He does this often. But not tonight. With the stick in his mouth, Jasper comes back to me, gets in his sit postion in front of my chair, and stares up at me. He is not going anywhere. I know it will not be long until the giant paws are pounding against my legs in rapid succession. Jasper's message is clear: "Get up. It will just be easier for you that way."

So, I get up. Immediately, he sprints out into the yard, taking a quick look back to make sure I'm coming after him. I am, but with a strategy in mind. In an effort to preserve my energy while still giving Jazz the feel of the chase, I move toward the middle of the yard. I am going to use this position so I can make a quick move toward him and then reset back to the middle once he reacts and races off in another direction. I can keep repeating the process until he is worn down. Should be fun.

But Jasper knows what's going on, so he darts right into the middle of the yard, putting the brakes on just before he is about to run into me. Back to the sit-and-stare position. He is trying to turn the tables on me. But not tonight: on this night, he will be going inside with his tail between his legs. This is serious business.

I stare right back at him and, without notice, make the charge. He is gone before I have even taken a full step. It doesn't matter—he has awoken a sleeping giant. I will catch him and take that stick right out of his mouth. Then, I will wave it in front of his face until he jumps for it, at which point I will pull it away. He will be biting thin air. It will be so satisfying as I repeat it over, and over, and over again.

Jasper heads toward a tree just a few feet in front of our patio and then comes to a stop. I am closing in on him. The only thing standing between me and that stick is one big tree trunk. It's a showdown, one that has occurred many times before. Jasper is positioned just enough to the side of the tree so that we can see each other. His eyes are locked on mine, inviting me to make a move. As always, they speak loud and clear: "Take your pick, buddy." Staring straight back at Jasper, I wait. My message could not be clearer: "Take *your* pick, tough guy."

Who is going to blink first? He knows who. But I sense Jazz has become overconfident. I have a plan, a brilliant plan. I will lean to his right, giving the appearance that I am about to chase after him from that side. But it will just be in preparation to break to his left, which is where Jazz will inevitably go as he sees the direction I am leaning. My thinking will be just a couple of seconds ahead of his, all the time needed to cut him off when he finally makes the decision to break left. I'll be standing in front of Jazz before he even knows what happened.

After a few seconds, I start to lean slightly to his right as planned. He watches intently. Nothing. A few more seconds go by. I lean in just a little more to his right. I can tell he is on the brink of making his break left. It's just so easy. But then, instead, he starts moving toward his right, inching closer to me. What is he doing? I wait. He moves closer still. The break left is just a second away. What a hole he has dug for himself.

But then, instead of making the quick move left, Jazz runs right at me. In a reflex reaction, I lunge for him. Too late. He is gone, leaving me in the dust, flat on my face. I can see him sprinting away. Then, the sprint turns into a happy, taunting trot, legs stepping high, his head bobbing up and down, the stick held firmly in his mouth visible from either side. There are no victory barks. He doesn't need them. I can hear what he is thinking: "You're looking a little bit dirty there, buddy. You might want to clean yourself up before you go inside—you know I like clean floors."

I get up and dust myself off. Jazz is now sitting in the middle of the yard chewing on his stick and watching me. So much for my master plan. I look back toward the patio and there's Marie standing at the screen door, laughing. She saw the whole thing. I can't help but laugh too. And just like that, my whole night has changed—from exhausted and not in the mood to do anything to laughing and alive. Jasper has done it again. Polar did the same thing in his own way. Now Jasper has taken the reins.

35 | DEPRESSION UNVEILED

For after all, the best thing one can do
when it is raining is to let it rain.
—Henry Wadsworth Longfellow

One evening I was sitting at the kitchen table, and Marie was standing about six feet away. She began to speak out loud about how excited she was about a major presentation Jack had delivered at school earlier in the day in front of parents and teachers. It was a grand slam.

Marie was so swept up in the moment that even as I was sitting in the same room with her and within speaking distance, it was as if she was speaking into the heavens with great joy about how all her hard work and effort had paid off. Given my inability to be fully present for so many years, I could understand why. I had not been a part of the picture for so long. It was not intentional, but nevertheless, that was the reality. Marie had worked tirelessly through the years to help Jack reach his full academic potential. And today was their day of victory.

Marie was beaming with pride. I may as well have been a ghost—I had missed pretty much everything. Depression had wiped me out. And at that very moment, it all hit me at once. Try as I did to hide it, I couldn't. On the evening of this very momentous occasion, tears suddenly began to stream down my face. They were not going to stop, and I did not want Marie to see what was about to happen. I headed straight for the powder room just off the kitchen. It was the right decision.

I sat down on the commode, put my cell phone on the floor, and let the tsunami of sadness fall over me. The tears poured out. I did not try to stop them. I just wanted to let all the pain and sorrow pour out of me—and did it ever. This episode was like nothing I had ever experienced. I went to reach for some toilet paper because my nose was running—no, it was gushing, as the tears continued streaming down my face. But then I hesitated, and instead of grabbing some toilet paper, impulsively I reached for my phone, pointed the camera at my face, pressed the button to take a selfie, and snapped the photo.

I was never one to take selfies. They didn't interest me. But this night, on the spur of the moment, I did. For the first time, I wanted to see what my face looked like during an onslaught of depression. When I finally settled down, I went outside to the back patio off of the kitchen and looked at the snapshot. It completely shocked me. It was tragic, devastating, and disgusting all at the same time. I thought to myself when I looked at my face—now, I truly know. Depression is real. It was the last piece of evidence—the real face of my depression. I needed to know it beyond a shadow of a doubt. And now I did.

I looked up at the sky through the branches of a tree and saw a full moon. I reached for my cell phone again and pointed it upward to take a snapshot. This time the decision was intentional. I wanted to capture what the sky looked like that same night. For some reason, it just seemed fitting to me to see the contrast between the face of my depression and the brightness of the full moon on a clear, Colorado night.

The fresh air did me some good. I took a deep breath and walked back in from the back patio, prepared to face Marie without breaking down. I wanted her to savor this night. She deserved it. As I closed the door behind me and walked back inside, the first thing I saw was Jasper, just lying on his bed, gnawing away at a stick he had snuck in from outside. It was a good feeling watching him. Exactly what I needed.

36 | TIME TO TELL JACK

Honesty is more than not lying. It is truth telling,
truth speaking, truth living, and truth loving.

—James E. Faust

It was 7:30 at night, and Jack headed straight upstairs to go to sleep. He was exhausted. Marie went up to his room to see how he was doing and say goodnight. I was right behind her. I hugged him, and as is the case every so often, he did not give me a full hug back. It was more of a sideways, half-hearted hug. And as was always the case, I put my arms around him and held him tight against my chest. No half hugs permitted where Jack was concerned. Marie and I both walked out of his bedroom, and he turned the lights off to get some rest.

Then, I stopped for a moment and thought. I had taken two sick days off from work and could sense it worried Jack. He had asked me earlier in the day if I had used up all my sick days. When I told him I had about one hundred and that I had only used three of them, I could see the relief on his face. I stood just outside his room for about two minutes and prayed. Was now the right time?

It had been just over three years since I had been an inpatient in the Highlands treatment center. I had always known that at some point, I would have to tell Jack what had happened, and why. He was thirteen years old when the event occurred—old enough to feel the fear, heartbreak, and anguish of not knowing what was happening to his dad—but still young enough that he could not possibly have any depth of understanding as to why. He deserved to know, and more importantly, he needed to know. And he had to hear it directly from me—just the two of us. I wanted Jack to understand everything about what had happened, why it had happened, and the things he should know to reassure him that I was well and doing everything necessary to stay well. The night was calm. I could hear Jack in my mind:

Why did Daddy have to go to the hospital?

Why did he abandon Mommy and me?

Is Daddy okay now?

Will he ever talk to me about everything?

Can I speak to him about it?

So many questions and concerns that I knew my boy had and always realized had to be answered. So, I turned around and walked back into his room. The lights were off, but his cell phone was on. The time had finally arrived.

"Jack, I want to talk to you. Do you have a few minutes before you go to bed?"

"Sure, Daddy," he replied.

I walked over and sat on the bed with him. I rested my hand just above his knee and said:

"Jack, I want to talk to you about what happened when I was in the hospital for a week. Do you know why I was in the hospital?"

"Depression," he replied.

"Yes, depression. But actually, it was major depression, and it was something I have dealt with for most of my life."

I instantly had his attention and could tell by the look on his face that he wanted to know everything. We talked for an hour, and I told him how I ended up in the mental health hospital, what it was like, how it ended up helping me, and the things I now have in place that enable me to enjoy life and stay healthy.

Jack listened intently, and I saw the tears welling up in his eyes. He was trying to hold them back, but he couldn't. I was saddened to see his sorrow, but felt relieved that he was able to release the pain and anguish that he must have been feeling for a long time. I am sure there are many more tears that will be shed and need to be. His healing had begun.

Jack is a highly intelligent, intuitive, caring, and loving person. He is one of those few people who really does have a heart of gold. Still, he is just sixteen years old and has been through an extremely traumatic experience. I could see and feel every bit of it as I walked him step-by-step through the moment I was involuntarily held in the hospital to everything I had done since that time to get better and stay better.

He asked questions along the way about different things he wanted to know more about, and I answered them directly and honestly with love and compassion. As I saw Jack's face slowly move from fear to sadness, to release of sorrow and grief, and finally ease back into a sense of calm, I stopped. After a brief pause, I asked:

"Jack, do you have any other questions?"

He looked away from me and said nothing. I waited, hoping I had reached a point at which he trusted me enough to ask anything that was on his mind. For a moment, it appeared as though he was going to say: "No." I would understand if he was not ready to ask questions that had to be on his mind. But then, he suddenly said:

"I really just have one question, Daddy. Are you going to off yourself?"

And there it was, all the questions that had to be swirling in his mind wrapped into one: "Are you going to off yourself, Daddy?" I thought to myself, what courage to be able to ask me that question.

And then I thought, through all the fear, pain, and grief I had put Jack through, he held no anger, and most, if not all, of the details he wondered about had been largely addressed. The one thing he needed to hear from me was that I would never take my own life.

Before Jack asked me that question, I had sometimes wondered myself if the depression would become too overwhelming again that it could threaten my life. But at that very moment, I realized my own son had just inoculated me from that possibility.

For the rest of my life, I will remember Jack asking that question, and me looking straight into his eyes and saying: "Never."

The look of relief on his face is vivid in my mind. It will remain there forever.

Thank God.

37 | ONE MORE TIME

Realize that you are not alone, that we are in this
together and most importantly that there is hope.

—Deepika Padukone

As I turn the corner, approaching the entrance, the parking lot comes into view. I was immersed in my thoughts for the fifteen-minute drive, thinking about how much has changed over the past four years. I find a space, turn into it, and shut off my car. Through the windshield, I see the building. Nothing has changed. My heart starts beating fast. I don't want to get out of the car, but there is no other option. As they say, the die is cast. It's time.

The walk to the front entrance is about a half a football field away, and my heart starts beating faster as I approach those glass doors. I already know they will be locked, so I wait just outside of them for the woman at the front desk to notice me. She is on the phone but glances up and sees me. I hear the buzzer and then a clicking sound. The lock is released. There is a very small window of time to open the door before

the lock falls back into place. Then, the second door. Another buzzer
followed by the clicking sound. The lock is released. Now my heart is
pounding through my chest as I enter the building and the door closes
behind me and I hear the lock fall back into place. In what feels like the
blink of an eye, I am sitting in the lobby at the Highlands for a second
time. How the hell did that happen? Something to think about while
I wait for the class leader.

Five months after my stay at the inpatient unit in the late fall of
2014, I had taken a job with a financial services firm as part of a team
of investment advisors. Yes, I said a financial services firm. Stop shaking

your head. Do you think I just went for the path of least resistance?

I had looked for opportunities outside of the industry because Sarah and I agreed that it would not make any sense to go back into a career that had played a part in how I ended up in the Highlands. But the reality was I had to get back to work, and all of my experience was in the financial industry. With that said, I did the best I could to find a job within the sector that Sarah and I believed I could handle. And it had to be in a culture that we were confident I could fit into. The position at this firm fit that criteria, and I was grateful to be offered the job.

The opportunity had opened up because one of the advisors on the team had recently left, and management was looking for a person they believed had the best background to fit the needs of the clients he was serving. Fortunately, that person turned out to be me.

After an initial training period, my work began. Suffice it to say, trying to take charge of my new responsibilities while still learning the company's systems was challenging for me. Thankfully, the team of people I was working with were all helpful and supportive. I had been given the tools and resources to succeed and was working with people who genuinely wanted me to succeed. This was unlike any other experience I had ever had in the industry. Perhaps I had finally found a home. Despite the reality that everything was moving in a positive direction, in my mind, failure was never far away, and financial ruin would be sure to follow.

This self-defeating mindset is one of the many gifts that is often a part of depression. In one of the classes at the Highlands, I learned about something called catastrophic thinking. It is a thought process that causes the mind to always take a person straight to the absolute worst-case disaster scenario. Having, over the years, become one of the elite catastrophic thinkers, without any rational thought about what actually might result from losing this job, I concluded that I would go bankrupt. Quite a leap. Yet this was the type of thought process I had perfected over the years. Sarah spent a lot of time helping me see how illogical and self-destructive this pattern of thinking was, but I clearly had more work to do to overcome it.

The consequence of thinking about my situation in this way—long nights, sometimes all night, agonizing over every bit of advice I would discuss with each client. Not exactly an optimal approach to completing my work, but my catastrophic mindset left me with no other choice. Get it right, or my world would fall apart. I was always just one wrong decision away from being broke. The way I was handling my responsibilities was unsustainable.

Enter Dr. Rachel Brooks. Like Sarah, Dr. Brooks was a referral from my church. When I first reached out to get an appointment, her voicemail said she was not taking on new clients at this time. I left my name, number, a little bit about my situation, and how I was referred to her. Figuring that was a dead end for who knows how long, it was back to the drawing board. Finding a psychiatrist I could have confidence in was not going to be easy.

A few days later and much to my surprise, I received a call from Dr. Brooks. She said that she would find a way to fit me into her schedule, and we set up an appointment to meet. The rest, as they say, is history. My first visits with her were reassuring. Dr. Brooks was compassionate, and I could tell she was committed to helping me in my recovery. But, as it turned out, she was way more than that.

Very early on, maybe my third or fourth appointment with her, Dr. Brooks noticed something that my previous, genius psychiatrist never did. I always had trouble staying focused on the topic we were discussing. During our conversations, I would often start looking at something else. She asked me to fill out a questionnaire. The results were conclusive. The diagnosis—ADHD, attention-deficit/hyperactivity disorder. Among the challenges for adults: time management, organization, prioritizing tasks, setting goals, and, as one could logically conclude, holding a job. As if that were not enough, it is now well-documented that a clear connection exists between ADHD and depression. Dr. Brooks prescribed Adderall. It was life changing.

The effects were immediate. My ability to focus and think with clarity increased substantially. Actually, for the first time in my life, I was able to do both. But the effects went well beyond that. The medication lifted the heavy weight of depression that had clouded my thought process going back to early childhood. It was a feeling of relief like I had never experienced before. I would even say—a miracle. And to think, eight years, twenty-three medications, and how about a jolt of ECT? For what? That's right, a one-week, all expenses paid vacation to the Highlands resort. Hard to believe, but I never wrote Dr. Hazel a thank-you note!

The one drawback to the Adderall: the effects were short-lived. After a couple of hours, the benefits topped out. Over the next hour or so, they gradually declined, and then over another hour, they faded away. Dr. Brooks once described it as a rainbow-type of effect—like a burst of color, curving higher, plateauing, and then rolling over and downward before fading away. It was life-altering while it lasted, but within four hours or so, I was back to square one. Still, the positive difference that drug made on my life was like nothing I had ever experienced.

With the Adderall in place and working, Dr. Brooks worked with me to find an antidepressant to directly address the depression. Because of my history, I was reluctant to try any, and on the first couple of recommendations, I had little tolerance for accepting any initial side effects. Dr. Brooks suggested that my prior experience was making it difficult for me to trust her and asked me to give her next recommendation a little more time to work, even if it meant trying to ride through initial side effects if they were to arise.

Dr. Brooks wrote me a prescription for Celexa. She explained that this antidepressant was known to be effective not just in treating depression, but also in treating anxiety disorders. She was confident I would do well on it. I understood her rationale and agreed to stick with it for as long as she advised me to.

The Celexa did not initially have any effect, but I stuck with it as promised, and sure enough, after about three weeks, I started to feel a slight improvement. The depression seemed to lift slightly, and my anxiety was not as intense. Over the next couple of months, both my depression and anxiety levels improved further. While my symptoms did not disappear, they were far better than they had ever been. The combination of the Adderall and the Celexa enabled me to become increasingly better at managing my workload. For the first time in my life, I was on a medication regimen that was beating back the depression.

Beyond finally getting me on a winning medication combination, Dr. Brooks helped me to gain a better perspective and understanding of the different challenges in my life that contributed to my depression. Between the medications, Dr. Brooks' ongoing guidance, and my therapy sessions with Sarah, things were finally starting to come together. It all seemed too good to be true—just a cruel head fake. My demise was just around the corner. It would be catastrophic.

With all the cylinders firing, I was getting into a rhythm at work. Three years after starting my job, the number of clients I was handling had risen, but the workload was manageable, and I was getting out of work at a reasonable hour and not taking any of it home. My life had become more balanced. For the first time in years, my life was more than just trying to stay afloat at work. It felt great to be fully engaged with Jack and Marie. I was present, not absent, with them and having fun. Jasper was a full member of our family. I always knew it was inevitable. Try as they might, there was simply no way Jack and Marie could ever resist the laughter and love he brought. He made it look easy. It all seemed too good to be true—and, as things turned out, it was.

Within about a month, give or take, there were some changes on our team. One of the outcomes of those changes was that I would be taking on some additional clients. Not a problem. I had room for growth in my practice, and by any measure, even with the additional clients, the workload was reasonable and manageable. At first, things were going smoothly as I began the process of reaching out to get to know the new clients I would be serving. It was all going as planned.

But within a few weeks, something changed. I started to fall a little behind. Nothing that was a cause for great concern, but it was happening. I just figured I would work my way through it. So, I stepped up my efforts, beginning to put in some extra time to accomplish what I needed to. I would be back on track in no time at all...But such was not the case.

Instead, with each passing day, I was losing ground. It didn't make any sense to me. I should have been able to handle the added responsibilities, but it was not turning out that way. What was happening? I didn't know, but I did realize that something was not quite right. Nevertheless, I charged ahead, taking whatever time was necessary to avoid getting too far behind on my workload. In no time at all I would be caught up and back on track. I had done this throughout my career, and I could do it again. Wrong. Yet again, I was back to the days of being wrong.

While this was unfolding, I was in ongoing communication with my manager. Patrick had always been supportive and encouraging. He gave me helpful guidance and always wanted to make sure I had the tools necessary to succeed. He was aware of the extra time I was putting in and that I needed to do some catching up. We discussed the current situation and came up with a game plan to get me caught up and back to the work-life balance I had achieved before. Unfortunately, what was happening was not going to be turned around with a game plan, no matter how good. Depression was making a comeback.

While I knew something didn't feel right as my struggles at work increased, what I didn't know was that it was depression that was responsible for it. I was also unaware of just how bad my condition had become. I was headed toward the fall of 2014 all over again. Dr. Brooks could see what was happening. She stepped in and put it all to a stop. Adhering to her orders, I would take a medical leave. Sarah was right with her all the way. Together, they rallied to my side, removing me from the situation and the inevitable tsunami of depression that was headed my way.

Dr. Brooks had a plan for the three-month leave. She wanted me to get on a new antidepressant, as in one that I had never tried before.

It was called a monoamine oxidase inhibitor—MAOI for short. It was the first-ever antidepressant, developed more than sixty years ago, and rarely prescribed anymore. But she said it was known to be highly effective in cases of depression that were resistant to treatment and also had properties that could take the place of the Adderall.

That is when Dr. Brooks explained the distinction between the rainbow effect of Adderall versus the steadier, ongoing focus, and motivating effects of this drug. Despite this drug's powerful properties, taking it came with strict dietary restrictions, ones that, if not followed closely, could lead to a sudden and sharp increase in blood pressure that could be life-threatening. For this reason, over the years, as newer antidepressants that did not have this side effect came to market, the use of an MAOI became rare. Still, there was never any question that this drug was quite effective in situations like mine. If I were willing to accept the dietary restrictions, Dr. Brooks saw my medical leave as an opportunity to transition to it.

The list of restrictions was quite long, but among the foods that were considered the most dangerous and to be avoided were: smoked or cured foods. Say goodbye to a rack of ribs. That would be a significant give-up. And bacon—a monumental give-up. On the flipside, there were some foods that I could live without. One was aged cheese—can't stand it. Fine by me. Quite a few alcoholic beverages such as red wine and beer containing yeast, typically from the tap, were also to be avoided. I don't drink, so no big deal. Overall, not too much of a sacrifice if this antidepressant worked as well as Dr. Brooks thought it might. It didn't matter anyway—she could have told me I would be limited to bread and water for the rest of my life. The decision would still be an easy one. I am serious.

Getting on this medication, however, was not a simple matter. It would entail a slow wind-down of the Celexa, followed by a period of going without it entirely. The same was true for the Adderall. Interactions between either of these two drugs and an MAOI were potentially fatal. We needed to proceed with caution. So, in the final phase of the transition process, there would be a period of time, Dr. Brooks said it could be as long as two weeks, that I would be without both medications. But there could be no other way. Further complicating the change was that the withdrawal from the Celexa, like others in its class of antidepressants, was known to have very unpleasant side effects. Suffice it to say, I would have to be under close supervision to make the change.

Dr. Brooks said I would have to be in an intensive outpatient program (IOP) while going through this transition phase. Sarah was of the same mind. I resisted. No thanks—those days were behind me. But it was not my choice. Without agreeing to enter the IOP, Dr. Brooks would not prescribe the new antidepressant.

So there I was, sitting in the Highlands lobby, about to start their outpatient program. It was just shy of four years since I first went there to learn more about it. Just a minor detour, but I finally was admitted to their intensive outpatient program. If nothing else, I never quit.

Suddenly, I heard the sound of the buzzer, and it was not coming from the entrance. A set of wooden double doors opened just behind and to the side of the front desk—it was the therapist who would be leading the IOP. She introduced herself, and then a group of ten to twelve of us got up and followed her back through the double doors. I heard them lock behind us as we started down a hallway on the way to our classroom. I remembered it well. The last time I was walking in the opposite direction. Just ahead, another set of wooden double doors. Our leader had the key card. The buzzer sounded again, they opened and on we went, passing the elevators that could take me one floor up to the inpatient unit. Tempting, but somehow, I managed to stick with the group.

We walked a short distance, and to our right, there was the cafeteria. I glanced at my table in the back—it was a walk down memory lane. Up ahead, another set of double doors. Another short buzz and as I looked down this next hallway, I saw glass doors at the end leading back outside. Locked, no doubt. Our classroom was the last one on the left before the exit. We followed the therapist into the room, and there were the tables just as I had remembered them, spaced together in the shape of a rectangle.

I sat down. Nobody was talking. Nobody looked at one another. It was like being on the New York City subway but in a quiet, uncrowded room. My chest was tightening. I just never expected to be here again. Just when I thought I had shaken it, my depression had returned. It was staring at me through about ten faces. The first time it happened almost four years ago, I felt a sense of relief. This time, I was humiliated.

I felt a wave of sadness, and wanted to get up and leave. But that was not going to happen. Within a few minutes, the therapist started the class. She introduced herself and then asked each of us to do the same. As each person spoke, something unexpected happened. My chest slowly relaxed, and the wave of sadness receded. I realized that I was back with friends. They may just as well have been the same group I went through inpatient with. It was a reunion of sorts. We all shared the same unique bond—depression.

On my own, the hopelessness of depression was frightening. But being in that classroom with people dealing with the same menace was uplifting. Shared misery? No, shared compassion and empathy. There was something so comforting and hopeful about being with my classmates. I was no longer alone. Just what I needed.

38 | WASTED TIME

Dig deep enough in every heart and you'll find it:
a longing for meaning, a quest for purpose.
As surely as a child breathes, he will someday wonder,
What is the purpose of my life?

—Max Lucado, *One God, One Plan, One Life*

Over the next several months, I made the long transition to the MAOI, but not without paying the price.

My withdrawal period from the Celexa was an opportunity for the depression to make a comeback, and it took full advantage of the situation. The worst was the anxiety. It took a hold of me within a week of starting my drawdown. And, as had always been the case, it was in full force from the moment I woke up after a deep sleep. My heart would be racing, pounding against my chest like it was hell-bent on bursting through it. The feeling was raw and intense, just as I had remembered it.

And then there was a side effect I had never experienced before—a sense of intermittent shocks. They were quick bursts. The sensation was similar to that tingling numbing feeling when you hit your funny bone, except it occurred in my head. There was no apparent trigger. They just happened. It got to a point where I was always on the alert, bracing myself for the next one. And then there was the irritability. It went through the roof and, unfortunately, Marie bore the brunt of it. By the end of the two-week withdrawal period, I was having second thoughts about moving forward with the transition, but I stuck with it. Dr. Brooks was confident the MAOI would do wonders for me, and I knew there would never be another opportunity like this one.

The Adderall was next. Having to eliminate the only medication that ever provided me real relief was the hardest part of the whole process. Adderall was a lifeline for me, but there was no turning back. I hung onto the hope of the MAOI and gave up the Adderall. The relief went with it. With both medications out of my system, and having tapered off of the Klonopin along the way, I was left with two weeks until I could start the MAOI. Perhaps it could have been shorter, but Dr. Brooks took great care to ensure my safety. She had my full trust, and I followed her lead.

So, now it was as if I were being placed on a high wire and was staring at a two-week walk between two cliffs without a safety net below. Being among friends in the IOP would play a large part in carrying me across. I made it, started the MAOI, and hoped for the best. For the first couple of weeks, the MAOI had no effect, and my leave of absence ended. It looked like the worst-case scenario. I told Dr. Brooks I had to get back on the Adderall. She encouraged me to give the MAOI a little more time. I was starting to have reservations about staying on course, but once again, I followed her recommendation. By the end of the third week, I began to feel a change, as the intensity of my anxiety diminished slightly. It was subtle, but real—I saw a glimmer of hope.

Over the next several weeks, I started to feel better and better. The MAOI seemed to be kicking in. It was difficult for me to believe; I was guarded. The possibility that I could ever find a medication that would rid me of depression had long since passed. Yes, the Celexa had been effective, but just enough to take the edge off of my depression. Believing that the MAOI would do much more was, I told myself, just wishful thinking.

Even as the MAOI was having a powerful effect, the idea that this would finally be the one was hard to believe, let alone accept. If I did, and it failed, then what? I had stared down the abyss of hopelessness once before. The second time would be the last. It would be depression's ultimate revenge. I shut down even the slightest hint of optimism.

But by the end of week eleven, there was simply no denying it: the first antidepressant ever developed would be the one to give me my life back. Five decades of suffering from depression, struggling to survive, and the medication I needed had been there all along.

It would be easy to think that I wasted all those years of my life when a solution was already at hand, but my thinking and emotions have matured. I believe that every experience has a hidden meaning, and every life has a purpose. It is up to us to find that meaning and discover that purpose.

I believe, with all sincerity, that this book will change people's lives. What more hopeful gift to give and receive than to turn your own life around in a positive direction, and then help others to do the same?

39 | CHARTING A NEW COURSE

You have brains in your head. You have feet in your shoes.
You can steer yourself any direction you choose.
You're on your own. And you know what you know.
And you are the guy who'll decide where to go.

—Dr. Seuss

By the early spring of 2019, I was managing my workload better than I ever had in my entire thirty-two-year career. I was up to an almost full slate of clients and getting things done within a normal workday. I was enjoying time at home with Jack and Marie and, of course, our canine comedian. A feeling that everything was going to be okay was gaining strength. And, with each passing day, the strength seemed to be building momentum. Yes. You heard me right. I said, "okay." Not exactly an enthusiastic description of what was happening, but it was a huge hurdle to let go of the fear that I would wake up one morning and feel the horrific anxiety again. I guess it was the final death-nail grip depression held on me—such an evil disease. But depression's nights were now numbered. The light was coming, and as the calendar turned toward the summer, I finally came to the realization that the battle had been won—goodbye, old friend. I will never miss you.

Looking back on five decades of depression, I know my victory can't change all of the life that depression has stolen from me. My moments of joy, like the birth of Jack, were stripped of their vibrancy. My laughter was never carefree. Sensations of pleasure were muted. Colors lacked their brilliance. And, worst of all, my capacity to love and be loved was greatly diminished. But through the gift of faith, the love and support of so many, and a sixty-year-old antidepressant, all that was stolen is not lost. My sense of optimism is being restored. I am undergoing a renewal. At long last, I can see possibilities.

It is late on a cool, breezy night. Earlier in the evening, though, there had been a big storm. Flashes of lightning and the rumbling sound of thunder filled the sky. There's nothing quite like the magic of a Colorado storm. Something soothing about them. All is calm now. Jack and Marie are asleep. Jasper, too. He is on our bed, curled up, with his back resting comfortably against Marie's leg. Something so satisfying about that. It took time, but she has taken Jasper into her heart—I always knew she would. Still awake, I decide to go out on our back patio and take in the beautiful night. The breeze feels so good. I sit in my chair and enjoy the moment. It is so quiet and peaceful. My mind is clear. So, I figure, why not? I close my eyes and start to think about the future.

For several minutes, there is nothing. It doesn't matter. It just feels good to be in such a relaxed, tranquil state.

And then, in an instant, I am standing somewhere in a vast, open space. There are wildflowers everywhere, and I can see the mountains far, far in the distance. I have no idea where I am, but the day is sunny and beautiful. I start walking, to where, I have no idea. After a few minutes, a pathway comes into view. It seems far away, but it must lead somewhere. Off I go walking faster and faster as I get closer to the path. I am there. Along the path, there is a river and lots of trees. The water is running fast, and the sound of it rippling over the rocks is soothing.

Turning a rounded corner of the pathway, I see what appears to be a crossroads. It is a long distance away, but there is nowhere else to go. I begin the long walk, and with each step forward, the view of the crossroads becomes clearer and crisper. I pick up the pace, a fast walk turning into a jog. The crossroads are now probably a quarter of a mile or so away. Increasing my speed, the jog turns into a run. Then a sprint. With the crossroads now clearly in my sights, I begin to slow down. I reach the intersection and stop right in the middle of it. A bit winded, I bend over slightly, placing my hands on my knees as I scan the area. Now what? Where am I? Where should I go? The roads look the same but take me in different directions. Which one?

Breathing easier, I straighten back up. I look to my left, then to my right, then ahead. Just three long dirt roads, nothing in sight in any direction. Maybe I should just turn around and head back. But to where? I am lost.

My heart begins to beat faster and pound against my chest. It feels natural, given the moment, just enough to keep me alert and nothing more. Then, I hear two voices off in the distance. They are faint, but I know them instantly. Looking back over my shoulder, I can start to see Marie and Jack coming into view. I hear them chatting and laughing together, all smiles as they stroll toward me. I had no idea Marie and Jack were anywhere near, but there they are, approaching me as if taking their time to catch up.

They wave to me as they approach. I smile and wave back, wondering where they came from. And, within no time at all, there they are, walking right up to me in the middle of the crossroads. Marie looks at me with her warm smile: "Hey, Bobby, where to now?" Her voice is caring and upbeat. Then Jack: "So where to now, Daddy?" His voice is happy; his face lit up with his trademark, chocolate chip cookie smile. I think to myself, both good questions, damned if I know. Better think of something fast.

And then, as I search for an answer, we all hear a noise off in the distance. Sure enough, it's him. Jasper is sprinting toward us with his "How could life possibly be any better?" expression on his face. We all turn around, excited to see him. "Hey, Jazz!" I shout, waving at him. He sees me waving and heads straight our way. Moments later, Jasper is running circles around us, breaking out of his loop every so often to bump into Marie or me or Jack. I should have known he would arrive just at the right time. Never could come up with a safe place to escape to if one of those therapy sessions with Sarah went south. So, instead, I took Jasper with me into each memory, and he became my safe place. It worked. He was always there when I needed him. Still is.

Jasper gradually settles down. He finds a stick, picks a spot on the grass just in front of us and starts chewing on it—a favorite pastime. He is quite content.

"So, Daddy, where are we going?" Jack is looking up at me, waiting for an answer. He, as usual, is ready to roll. No more waiting. I look back at him, then glance over at Marie. She is ready to get moving, as well. So, there we are. Together. A family.

Something is missing, though—Polar. I think about Polar often and sometimes wonder if he ever thinks about us. The answer is always the same: of course he does. After all, he is the Great Connector. Polar is a part of all of us, so he is here with us. Just as it always should be.

And then, suddenly, it hits me. Even though I had disconnected from the world long ago, Marie had never let go of me. She was always there, and so was Jack. She kept us together. Even through the darkest days, Marie never left my side. She had walked with me every step of the way. Why, I will never fully understand. But I am grateful that she did.

"Alright, Jack, you want to know where we're going? Well, you're about to find out. Just follow me." And with that, I reach out, taking Jack's hand with my left and at the same time, Marie's with my right. I hold them both tightly. "You ready, Jazz?" He looks up at me with a stick still in his mouth and waits for what's next.

"Okay everybody, here we go."

"Which road?" I think to myself, taking the first step forward. And then I realize it no longer matters. Whichever road I take, the journey will be with them, guided every step of the way by the bright light of hope.

Each story has an ending
—some happy, some sad, some heroic.

It is my hope that by having read this book
and confronting the issue of depression head-on,

Someone's story will change for the better,
and they will find that happy ending
and become the hero
of their own life.

CLOSING MESSAGE | HOPE

It has been a privilege to share my story with you. As I said from the very beginning, depression remains, for far too many people, an extremely difficult subject to discuss openly.

My greatest hope is that, by taking the journey through these pages you feel like it may be easier, even if it is just a little bit, to speak freely about this disease.

I truly believe that ridding the world of the stigma associated with depression, more than anything, will dramatically change the lives of those suffering from this disease, as well as their family and friends, for the better.

Always remember that you are not alone. There are millions of people just like you, struggling with depression. There are millions more willing to do whatever they can to help you get better.

Please let them help you. Each one of them is a light of hope. And there is hope.

My five-decade journey is just one testament, among millions, that there is always hope.

POSTSCRIPT | THE JOURNAL ENTRY

I only made one journal entry over my one-week stay at the hospital. Looking back, it was really the only one I needed. On my third night, just before lights-out for bedtime, I picked up my miniature golf pencil, and the rest came out naturally.

SUNDAY, NOVEMBER 16, 2014

I just got to thinking about my experience thus far and am amazed at what has transpired. When I came to the Highlands Mental Behavioral Health Center on Friday, I was just looking for information. Three hours later, I was being told I could not leave. In a word: shocking. I was then told that they were putting me on a "72-hour watch." I had two choices. I could sign a form stating that I would voluntarily check into the Center, or I would be checked in on an involuntary basis. Either way, I was staying. I was in no condition to read through all my rights. I was taken involuntarily.

Absolutely crazy. I cannot remember how I got from the office to my bedroom, but here I am—what a trip. Having to call Marie to tell her has to be the hardest thing I have ever done in my life.

Maybe this will be the turning point in my life. I have been fighting the depression demons as far back as I can remember. They almost got the best of me, but no more. Their time in my head, my body, my life is gone. Forever.

And by the way, as I lie here writing, I cannot help but think of the other special people I have met who are fighting similar battles. They are good people. They understand my fight, and I understand theirs. I just met them, and yet it seems like at least to some degree, I know them. An invisible bond that ties us together that only we can understand.

The mystery of depression. What a blessing to be with them.

BE STEADFAST |
A MESSAGE FROM MARIE

WORDS OF ENCOURAGEMENT
FROM MY WIFE

This is difficult to sit down and write. I don't like to talk about it. I think a lot of people are like me and don't want to talk about depression. In fact, I *know* that a lot of people are like me. For me, it's just uncomfortable. I have never felt that a depressed person is weak. Quite the contrary.

Here it is, a small window into how I have come to this new place of hope with Bobby.

How do I summarize twenty-eight years of a marriage when I didn't even know my spouse was deeply depressed? Looking back, there were clues. Then, eventually, the clues became my new reality. Bobby has somehow always carried this family, even when he couldn't get out of bed. He's the strong one. Yet, so many little telltale signs occurred, but I missed them. Until the day came that I had no choice but to face the fact that my life wasn't ever going to be the same. But what was the same? I was the one living in an alternative universe. My husband was in a dark place, and I didn't even see it coming. There were calls to ambulances for an illness, a "heart attack," a bad reaction to a cancer medication, and so on. And I still missed it. My husband was suffering horribly, and I couldn't see it. It was time for me to focus on helping Bobby from the disease called depression.

I have summarized a few areas that have helped me. I don't know if it will help you, but one thing I do know is that you will see that you are not alone after reading this book.

I don't have to tell you what a toll depression takes on people. But hold steadfast because that will ultimately help you win, in my opinion. It could take years. But you will win by working together with therapists, family, friends, religious leaders, strangers and, of course, each other.

Here are my takeaways:

Be an advocate for your family member. Triple check the doctors and/or facilities that you may be considering for your loved one.

Be on alert! Be a protector of your family member. It's easy for them to be taken advantage of by anyone!

Understand that it's critical that your family member is rested, eats healthy, and practices self-care. Help them accomplish these things as much as you can.

Talk to other people who are in the same situation as you are, or who you trust to just listen to you. The more you can help yourself, the more you will be able to help your family member.

Be open to what your depressed family member has expressed that they want. In our case, it was getting a family dog, which I highly recommend. (I can't believe I just wrote that!)

Don't ever give up. I know you won't quit on your family member, otherwise you wouldn't be reading this book!

Sometimes your family member just needs you to physically be there. You don't have to say anything. Just be there. Maybe touch them reassuringly.

A combination of these points, along with others, brought my family to a place of hope.

There is hope. You aren't alone.

Be steadfast.

Let go of the past and go for the future.
Go confidently in the direction of your dreams.
Live the life you imagined.

—Henry David Thoreau

ACKNOWLEDGMENTS

This book would not have been possible without the guidance and input of some extremely talented people.

To Coach David Strauss, thank you for leading me through the process of writing this book from start to finish. Simply pulling the story out of me was a major hurdle, yet you found a way. And thank you for bringing structure to the story, and for your ideas and suggestions that added to the book. Thanks also for keeping me on track and focused—well, way more than anybody else could. How you ever did it will always be a mystery to me. I am so grateful for your support during the difficult periods I went through in writing this book. And, perhaps most of all, thank you for never quitting on me!

To Aaron Sullivan, thank you for bringing your editing skills to this project. Your questions and comments helped to bring this story together.

Thank you, Diane Stockwell, for bringing better clarity and continuity to my writing. And thank you for caring about this story. I am so fortunate that you became a part of this project.

To Michael Ferguson, thank you for bringing your enormous talent to this project. Your illustrations are such an important part of this story, and the thoughtfulness and care you gave to getting every moment just right meant so much to me. This book would not be the same without your amazing work!

Love always to my wife Francesca Marie. I would not be here without you and this book would never have been written but for your love and support. I will forever remember the night when I could not see a way forward with this book. Too many scrambled notes and random thoughts on mixed up papers. But you believed in the importance of this story and knew better than me that I had to write it. You somehow were able to organize all of those notes and papers. Because of what you did that night, this story has come to life.

And to my son Jack, thank you for your 1:00 a.m. and 2:00 a.m. visits while I was writing this book. They always re-energized me. And I owe you a debt of gratitude for making sure I saved all my work in multiple places. You know me too well! I love you more than you will ever know.

To Mom and Dad, one of the most important things I have come to realize through my years of struggling with depression is that everybody is hurt by it, but nobody is at fault. Please know, I am truly thankful for all you have given me in life. Your support and love have never wavered. Such an incredible gift. I love you with all my heart.

Thank you, Cathryn, for always being a loving and supportive sister. The talks we had from time-to-time while I was writing this book always made me feel better. I love you.

Thank you, Jeff, for giving Francesca Marie, Jack, and I a special night we will always remember together. There will never be another New Year's Eve like 2016. I love you brother.

To Dennis Engel, Stephen Abrams, and Don Salcito: thank you for the many great times and never-ending laughter you have brought into my life. I am so thankful for your friendship.

Thank you Dr. Shandra Wilson for all you have done for me through the years. I am grateful for our friendship and blessed that you have been a part of my life.

To Jason Halko, your compassion and understanding before, during, and after my medical leave meant so much to me. Thank you.

To the exceptional people I met while being a part of the Outpatient Treatment Program at the Highlands, every one of you is an inspiration to me: Gretchen, Brooke, Sharon, Emma, Sandy, and Jay. I am grateful for the time we shared together.

To the exceptional people I met during my stay at the Inpatient Treatment Program at the Highlands, thank you for playing a part in giving me a second chance in life: Lauren, Candace, Olivia, Paul, Heather, Austin, and Warren. I am grateful for the time we shared together.

To Dr. Sarah Warren, thank you for your expertise, support, and guidance. I am grateful for all you have done for me.

To Mary Braun-Payne, your faith in God guided me out of a state of hopelessness. Your unwavering belief in the healing power of Christ gave me hope that I could recover.

Special thanks to Highlands Behavioral Health. Because of the treatment I received under your care, I was able to begin to heal and start down the long road to recovery. I am here today because of you and am forever grateful.

ABOUT THE AUTHOR

BOBBY STRAUS is a public speaker and author of *In Search of a Way Out: A True Story of, Bullying, Depression, and a Journey Toward Hope*. In this uplifting story, Bobby shares private details of his decades-long struggle to overcome depression to give the millions that are suffering, and their families, the hope that recovery is possible and the comfort and relief of knowing that they are not alone. In support of organizations dedicated to building awareness about mental health, Bobby offers his time to the National Alliance on Mental Illness (NAMI), as one of their speakers giving hope to patients in mental healthcare facilities, families of those caring for loved ones suffering from depression, students and staff in high schools and universities, and more.

Bobby has spent more than thirty years working in the financial markets as a trader, professional money manager, and investment advisor. Along the way, he has made appearances on CNBC and has been quoted in the Wall Street Journal, New York Times, Barron's, and Fortune Magazine. Bobby has been a speaker in the finance industry for many years. He has earned a BA in journalism from New York University and an MBA from the University of Denver. Bobby lives in Colorado with his wife, son, and their canine comedian, Jasper.

You can learn more about Bobby at www.bobbystraus.com

He can be reached via email at bobby@bobbystraus.com

You can write to Bobby at:

5910 S. University Blvd., Suite C - 18, Box 115

Greenwood Village, Colorado 80121